Cosmic Uplink

First Edition 2010

Published by
Ravi Dhariwal for the proprietors,
Bennett, Coleman & Co. Ltd.,
New Delhi

Edited, Designed, Marketed & Distributed by

Times Group Books

Times Group Books
(A division of Bennett, Coleman and Company Limited)
Times Annexe, 9-10, Bahadur Shah Zafar Marg, New Delhi-110002

Printed at: Saurabh Printers Pvt. Ltd.

ISBN 978-81-89906-91-7

Price: Rs.295

Send your feedback at: editor.tgb@timesgroup.com

Contents

FINE-TUNING SELF 42

Preface

A WRITER-FRIEND FROM Bollywood once compared the preface to a bridal veil or *ghunghat*. It neither hides nor completely exposes the contents. It is something one gets past quickly, to check out all that brightness and beauty shining within. "But that's in reel life (as in real life too)!" you might protest. "What about this preface? What does this first-ever anthology of 'Cosmic Uplink' columns from the edit page of *The Economic Times* have to offer?"

How about starting with cool connectedness to dimensions other than those that power and self provide? Please also include insights and explorations of realms spiritual, secular and scientific if you like. And don't forget tools and techniques for a fuller and more empowered life for everyone.

To return to the *suhag raat* or our conjugal metaphor, 'Cosmic Uplink's' ultimate design can be compared to that of the vows (no pun intended) of the Indian marriage: These seek fulfillment for those who consent to abide by it in all four quadrants of human endeavour or *purushartha*. These range from *artha* (money or meaning) and dharma (law, rules) to *kama* (desire or goals) and *moksha* (liberation and freedom).

Also, like the Milk-Testing Swan of Indian poetry, 'Cosmic Uplink' strives to sift the transient from the essential to offer a wealth of insights drawn from a variety of sources and experiences, from the most contemporary to the most timeless.

When it first appeared in an avatar called 'Spiritual Quotient', the core constituency of the column was the vibrant fraternity of ET readers. Naturally, this included movers and shakers, and the crème de la crème of business, finance and tech-savvy enterprise wherever ET, as one of the world's most respected and coveted business papers, is read.

Like its parent paper, 'Cosmic Uplink' which began as an innovation, quickly acquired a devoted following in both virtual and real realms. Clippings began to coalesce into personal collections and in blogs and on networks. Enquiries about 'Cosmic Uplink' between covers started pouring in.

To lift the veil further, the present volume brings together some of our more stimulating offerings. Just go ahead and enjoy yourself! Feel free to browse at your own pace and leisure. Each piece is meant to stand alone. Yet each is connected to the others, and to you, and ultimately to the entire world beyond. We do hope you will have as much fun and as many Aha moments as we have had in putting this together for your pleasure.

Vithal C Nadkarni
Mumbai
July 2010

Introduction

THE WRITINGS IN this volume may strike as esoteric to some people. Thought-provoking certainly they are, but none of them is beyond the ken of any serious reader. Selected from the 'Cosmic Uplink' column published in *The Economic Times* on all days except Sundays, the write-ups are intended not so much to entertain as to make the reader reflect on different issues — both perennial and topical.

The book has been divided into four sections: 'Blissful Living', 'Fine-Tuning Self', 'Transcendental Thoughts' and 'We & Science'.

The first section, 'Blissful Living', is based on the tenets of the Vedic scriptures which say that it is human nature to be in a state of bliss and everything on this Earth is aimed at helping us (the divine creatures) to achieve this. The articles culled in this section emphasize on joyous living, righteous attitude, gratitude, etc. The cornerstone is that one should seek inner happiness which is everlasting.

Write-ups in the chapter 'Fine-Tuning Self', centre around the theme of self-improvement and self-motivation — mantra for success in today's life. Some of the articles are about having the right attitude, living in the present, being clear about one's priorities, etc. The theme of this section revolves around success in life for which we not only have to be talented but also require right attitude. And all this comes only with fine-tuning the self. Through allusions and anecdotes from religious texts the articles give us the liberty to choose the path to succeed in life.

The sections following 'Fine-Tuning Self' might have a restricted appeal — it is meant for the highbrow as articles in both the sections 'Transcendental Thoughts' and 'We & Science' reflect on issues which are not simple. 'Transcendental Thoughts' presents issues which are beyond the realm of the ordinary day-to-day living. The write-ups that appear in this section take us through the personal experiences of immortals and anecdotes and give a peek into what transcendental living or thought is.

'We & Science' tries to explain both the simple and the complex scientific concepts. It not only tries to unravel the mysteries of the universe but also explains how human creativity is behind the changes that we see around us. The last two sections pose questions about the transcendental and sciences which might be a subject of debate.

Blissful Living

The Vedas say that we are divine creatures whose true nature is bliss and that we are born to enjoy the bounties of this wonderful world. The scriptures also say that to enjoy blissful living one should look for joy within oneself. And only when one looks for joy within that he/she experiences true bliss, which ultimately leads to enlightenment. This is the main theme running through the articles appearing in this section.

A life of bliss can be attained by practising virtues like contentment, poise, clarity and goodness. But people take to evil ways which prove to be materially rewarding in the short-term but lead to disaster in the end.

All religions of the world recommend particular paths to be followed by the seekers of truth. At the same time, they point to the evil ways which must be shunned. While enumerating the concept of *yama* and *niyama*, Patanjali's *Yoga Sutra* also identifies ten 'obstacles' to yoga.

The ancient Chinese philosophy of Taoism says that a blissful life flows with the nature and that only when we consider ourselves to be part of nature and start feeling one with it do we attain bliss.

In one of the articles where Swami Shankarananda talks about education he calls conventional education as First Education or Knowledge. The other he calls Second Education or Wisdom Tradition which goes to say true happiness lies within.

The modern man drives himself to desperation in pursuit of ephemeral things but misses out on the real joy of living. The bottom line is: Life is God's greatest gift to mankind and it ought to be lived blissfully.

Shed Your Worries to Float Across

Vithal C Nadkarni

AT THE PREDAWN hour, the City of Light on the Ganga looks a little like the Queen of the Night by the Arabian Sea, from where your columnist had flown in with a Dutch scribe. As our boat churns through the sacred waters off Benares, there is a whoosh and a glittering submarine form glides by the prow. "Sisu!" the boatman hisses.

"Does he mean a corpse?" whispers the scribe, who lives on a boat in a city famed for its carmine-coloured 'cannonball' cheese.

In response the boatman puckers up the fingers of his right palm into a cobra-like hood and makes dolphin-like curving, dancing movements. "Of course he means the dolphin," the penny drops. Sisu is the local name of the Gangetic Dolphin, which marine biologists have woven into the creature's Latin name as well. There is another splash and the dolphin tumbles by the side of our boat once again.

This time the *darṣhan* is long enough for us to spot its tiny vestigial eyes. These make it look like some myopic Muni grinning perpetually with its half-open beak-like mouth. The facts are more prosaic: over millions of years of the Sisu's evolution in the muddy environment of the Ganga, its eyes have withered away and the dolphin is not grinning as much as sending waves of sonar to 'see' its way around.

We must regard ourselves as fortunate for having seen so highly endangered a creature so quickly. "Perhaps there's a more ominous portent to the encounter," the scribe begins to ruminate uneasily. "Aren't dolphins traditionally regarded as porters of the dead?" They are indeed. Notice how William Butler Yeats used them in his celebrated poem 'Byzantium'; where after 'dying into a dance/ an agony of trance' the poet arrives into the city of eternity 'astraddle on the dolphin's mire and blood' by that 'gong-tormented sea'.

We decide to ask the boatman, "What kind of *shakun* (omen) is the Sisu?"

"*Ji Shubh!* (Lucky)," he replies.

Is he certain? What if our boat were to capsize now? Does he have life-jackets for us all? In response to our persistent questioning, the boatman simply quotes a *doha* from Kabir, the 15th century mystic master who was connected with the City of Light (Kashi).

The couplet is about a worn-out boat (*nab jarjari*) rowed by a frail old captain: "Travel light (without worries) if you want to float across," the master advises, "(*halke halke tire*). For those who loaded their heads, sank (*Bude tini sirh bhar*)."

Good Life Involves Pleasure & Virtue

Vithal C Nadkarni

IN *TROY*, HOLLYWOOD'S recent retelling of an ancient fracas, Orlando Bloom, who plays Paris, gets to keep his prize — Helen played by Diane Kruger. In this version the playboy prince is not killed by Philoctetes but is shown leaving the burning city of Troy with Helen. He lives to fight another day. The ending may seem unexceptionable for our 'liberated' times. But earlier versions all had Paris getting his 'just deserts'.

However, was Paris really to blame for his alleged crime of passion? Didn't Goddess Aphrodite promise him the love of the world's most beautiful woman in exchange for the golden apple?

The Goddess of Discord Eris originally created the golden globe inscribed with the words 'to the fairest' out of pique for not having been invited to a marriage party on Mount Olympus! She then tossed it into the party and watched the fun as three powerful goddesses fought over the fruit. Rather than risk the ire of the losing parties, the gods passed the potato to Paris who was known for his artless honesty.

It's another matter that the shepherd-turned-prince was so besotted by beauty that he did not bother to read the fine print — Helen was already married to the powerful King Menelaus who had the backing of dozens of warrior-princes. So would Paris have been better off in choosing brains instead of what the Goddess Athena promised along with skill in war in lieu of the apple? Or should he have been more impartial and chosen Hera, arguably the most beautiful of the three goddesses, who promised him kingdom of Asia and Europe for the apple?

A bigger question relates to binary stereotypes and puritanical mind-sets that tend to pit beauty against brains or pleasure versus duty and virtue. Why couldn't Paris have the option of choosing beauty with brains? That is the thesis of AC Grayling's latest book *The Choice of Hercules* which starts with the Greek hero who said 'no' to a life of ease and chose the greatly harder life of a lion-killer mercenary and stable-cleaner.

Grayling argues however that in the original Epicurean ideal, pleasure and virtue are not at all mutually exclusive. Nastily effective religious propaganda separated the two. In fact, the 'good life' should involve both, and by identifying one's strengths and behaving in a sensible, courteous fashion, you can get onto that 'middle path'. Have the flashy Ferrari along with the freedom of the monk.

Honesty is Indeed the Best Policy

K Vijayaraghavan

BENJAMIN FRANKLIN'S OBSERVATION that 'vicious actions are not hurtful because they are forbidden but are forbidden because they are hurtful' enables the intelligent seeker to comprehend why established religions and faiths are bound by the common factor of advocating virtuous acts and forbidding unhealthy actions and thoughts.

Corrupt and evil acts could perhaps be materially rewarding and also sometimes offer titillating sensuous pleasures but would also bring with them burdens and entanglements, whereby the person concerned would be cornered into a state where he would find that all ill-gotten accumulations finally prove to be nagging liabilities.

In contrast, he would also divine how simple virtues of contentment, clarity, poise and goodness would continually nourish his spirit that with intelligence, perseverance and application, his needs and wishes — including the materialistic and the mundane — would also be fulfilled. Radiating also peace, joy and succour for all around, he would thus be confronted by win-win situations all over.

Particular virtues to be followed and specific issues to be avoided are conceived of by different faiths and religions and also by the concepts of *yama* and *niyama* of Patanjali's *Yoga Sutra* and his enumeration of the ten 'obstacles to yoga' (1, 30). The ultimate manifestation of freedom from all afflictions is that state of freedom from self-centredness. This verily is that supreme freedom which, as Norman Vincent Peale notes, generates 'a kind of ecstatic joy and delight in living'. This also is the process of living out the age old Sanskrit concept of *vasudaiva kudumbakam* or *atmavat sarva bhooteshu*. True happiness and peace, indeed, are the rewards of such caring and empathy!

This also is discovery of that integration or yoga within, which *Bhagavad Gita* observes (6, 23) is 'dissociation from all suffering'. This integrity, through cementing the right virtues of head and heart within, generates invariably that abiding honesty and wholesomeness. Actually, through this process and methodology, the person does a singular service to himself, where he is the principal beneficiary. Truly, therefore, such an approach is, thus, not based on any morbid rhetoric, philosophy, self-abnegation or moral preaching, but on pure, simple and practical considerations for one's own welfare and true enjoyment — both in the short-term and the long-term. Indeed honesty is the best and most rewarding policy!

Fly Off to Your Virtuous World

K Vijayaraghavan

ONE'S PERSONALITY IS essentially and eventually the sum total of his different traits — the positive and negative. In this manner, each person's character is shaped and this manifests through his thinking, actions and approach, thereby also the circumstances and situations which attend on him. His destiny is thus ultimately fashioned. Character is thus the base from which everything issues forth. This is the concept of 'character ethic' of Stephen Covey, which is fundamental to human happiness and fulfilment.

Cultivation of virtues, dear to heart, naturally also goes with shunning the opposites of these and to 'shrink from these as something more terrible than fire', in the manner conceived of by the great Tamil bard Valluvar (Kural, 202). Bhagavad Gita (6, 5) also urges the seeker to uplift himself by his own self without permitting debasing influences to affect him.

The following exhortation in the Bible (Philippians - 4, 8) is highly inspiring in this regard: "Whatsoever things are true, whatsoever things are honest, whatsoever things are just, whatsoever things are pure, whatsoever things are lovely, whatsoever things are of good report; if there be any virtue, and if there be any praise, think on these things'.

Stephen Covey also refers to Benjamin Franklin's cultivation of his character. An analysis of Franklin's autobiography and the thirteen virtues, which he assiduously cultivated, would reveal how such an approach is primarily directed towards one's own benefit and not out of consideration for others or for reaping rewards in his next world. Religions and faiths therefore urge upon man to be righteous, virtuous, kind and good — the process which would ultimately ensure that he becomes the principal beneficiary. As Franklin observes, 'vicious actions are not hurtful because they are forbidden, but forbidden because they are hurtful'. He notes that it is, therefore, in everyone's interest to be virtuous if he wished to be happy even in this world.

The sense of fulfilment attendant on virtue is summed up in Addison's Cato, as quoted by Franklin:

"If there is a power above us
(And that there is, all nature cries aloud
Thro' all her works),
He must delight in virtue,
And that which he delights in must be happy".

As noted by Alexander Pope:

"Know then this truth (enough for men to know),
Virtue alone is happiness below".

Indeed, flying off to a virtuous world is also flying off to one's own joyful and rewarding world too!

Too Positive For One's Own Good?

Vithal C Nadkarni

AS ECONOMIES AROUND the world threaten to melt and ooze like Salvador Dali's surrealist clocks, groves of academe are agog with whispers about positive psychology. John Mayer, who teaches psychology at University of New Hampshire, for instance, asks in his blog if financial caution was undone by positive thinking. "The gust of contentedness that psychological treatments promote in contemporary society is unparalleled," he adds. "We have unlocked a Pandora's box of psychic positivity — perhaps without fully understanding its ramifications."

Of course, this is hardly the sort of stuff that fuels burnings at the stake. Nobody is out on a witch-hunt yet and the subprime crisis is still to be equated with the prime time devoted to positive psychology. The movement urges healers to zero in on people's strengths rather than weaknesses, and it implicitly advocates a benign neglect of the darker sides of the psyche.

"To be sure, positive thinking would be — at most — one among many causes of the financial decline," Dr Mayer concedes. "There have been financial declines many times before the advent of treatments to reduce negative thinking. Moreover, some contend that despite such treatment advances, depression is on the rise," he continues. "But could it be that by failing to contend with negative information, matters get worse and cause more depression?"

Dr Mayer has a point, which has also been eloquently made in the Indian tradition. The great mystical poet philosopher Sri Jnanadeva, for example, illustrates our failure to contend with negative information with the parable of the bull that goes out to graze in tiger country: A zebu forced to eke out a living from overgrazed commons became greatly discontented. Unbeknown to its master, the bull strayed into the forest that bordered the little village.

Here the bull found luscious grass and aromatic herbs growing in great abundance. But the hungry animal failed to notice the chilling silence that hung over the forest. Even monkeys and crows had fled due to the rank smell of a huge tiger that lived in a bamboo brake nearby.

Fortunately, the tiger wasn't at home. So the animal fed happily, drank from a forest pond and went home without noticing the huge pug marks of the tiger all around the rim. Next day, the bull happily returned to the forest still unaware of danger. With negativity, it might have lived.

Happiness is the Next Model

Mukul Sharma

"THE PRICE WE pay for our advance in civilization is a loss of happiness," wrote Sigmund Freud. Does this mean pleasure and progress don't go together? On the face of it, this doesn't appear to be so considering the benefits of technology, which we have reaped, have generally upped our quality of life. The wheel gave us increased and easy mobility, agriculture reduced dependence on foraging, printing extended the reach of knowledge, antibiotics alleviated suffering, electronics has revolutionized communication and entertainment. Surely, such palpable gains cannot have contributed to a loss of happiness?

Statistics bear this out too. Researchers at Britain's University of Leicester developed what they call the first 'World Map of Happiness' a couple of years ago using a battery of data, plus the subjective responses of 80,000 people across 178 countries. According to them the most significant factors were health, the level of prosperity and access to basic education. Not surprisingly, Denmark and five other European countries aced the list while Zimbabwe and Burundi scraped the bottom.

Freud, however, was talking about a totally different kind of unhappiness — the one that results from the constant pursuit of pleasure as a by-product of societal and technological development. He meant the more there is on offer, the more is desired by people, so that when supply understandably fails to meet demand, it breeds discontentment. How this has occurred is not difficult to see. Once upon a time what civilization offered in the form of advances were tools and choices that made human activity easier. This slowly turned to offering lifestyles that had the potential to change patterns of living and behaviour. What has happened from about the time Freud made his observation is that happiness itself is perceived as being on offer.

This has brought about a subtle shift in people's attitudes. They begin to believe that happiness is some sort of birthright that needs to be addressed until it's achieved. It ultimately boils down to the next model of an MP3 player, car, house, job, travel destination, diet plan, Botox technique, self-help book or yoga class. Unfortunately, as the Buddha too discovered long ago, the next model is always out of stock in the present. Thus, unavailability leads to disenchantment and only desire remains. What could be an unhappier condition?

Right Attitudes Can Ignite Latent Energy

Vithal C Nadkarni

WHETHER IT'S THE Incredible Hulk or Iron Man, comic-book action heroes are in great form. Now comes yet another avatar: Will Smith's Hancock is a superhero so psyched up by his 'unwanted' powers that he zonks around his rescue missions in a state of half-inebriation. "More often than not, he creates more problems than he solves," says a reviewer. "No wonder his public boos him. He is, inevitably, based in Los Angeles, where image is all, and his image desperately needs a makeover."

That's when the superhero runs into an image consultant whom he saves from certain death. The spin-doctor returns the favour by taking on the reluctant superhero as his client. In this sense, most of today's action stars, including the newest version of Batman, are all unwilling custodians of their powers. The clean-cut boy-next-door type of gung-ho do-gooders that you once saw in comics and on screen have been replaced by angst-ridden anti-heroes who would gladly junk their costumes and hide their powers for a 'normal' life with wife and kids. Their message is that superheroes are people, too — only more so.

But then people don't just go to theatres to watch folks one can meet in the mirror. They still root for stars with planet-shaking powers. Arjuna, for all his angst before Kurukshektra, for example, still retains his heroic spirit even when Shiva disguised as a tribal hunter, literally grinds the great warrior into dust in the epic Kiratarjuneya.

In the end it's all about possibilities and potentials waiting to be ignited by right attitudes and actions. The heroic myth holds out the promise of a cosmic order willing to accommodate all too-mortal courage. This is what Shiva does when the blue-throated Lord pretends to quarrel with the Pandava prince who is seeking the supreme Pashupata weapon with staggeringly fierce austerities.

Now how could a mere mortal even imagine that he could fight such an opponent? Yet Arjuna unknowingly does precisely that and is beaten to pulp for his hubris. Still, he refuses to give up and fashions a *linga* from the mud in which he's grovelling, to worship it with his tears of wrath. As he prays for strength, a miracle happens; the flowers that Arjuna places on the icon fly to head of his adversary who is all pleased to restore the battered hero to glorious strength. Now that's the kind grace-under-pressure which has been a bestseller in every age.

True Happiness Lies Within

Vithal C Nadkarni

THE MEMORY OF the catheter winding its way silently up an artery, brings to mind the words of Swami Shankarananda: "We are the most educated and affluent people in human history." The mystic who studied under Baba Muktananda writes in *Happy For No Good Reason*: "We can replace one person's heart with another's, we can fly people to other planets, and we can send tiny cameras into people's organs to inspect them from within. We are able, or will be able, to do almost anything in the physical world. However, we find this world stressful and demanding."

How true, the scribe shudders silently, recalling the memory of the dye seeping warmly through his innards. It reminds him of the sheer terror of unknowingness of what he'd always taken for granted was his own body. "We have trouble motivating our teenagers and keeping them away from negative influences. We find it difficult to control anger, fear or depression. We are confused by the world within ourselves." Now he's telling me, the scribe mutters to himself recalling the grave message in the angiogram.

But the scribe also recalls being simultaneously in the grip of elevating epiphany: this is too transient to be truly true! As if on cue Swami Shankaranada seems to concur in the following paragraph: "Our situation becomes intelligible if we recognize that we live in two different worlds simultaneously." Before getting into the cath lab, the scribe had described the same thing to his significant other with the help of the index finger of his right hand pointing towards her with the thumb stretched back towards himself. "The outer (*bahar*) and the inner (*antara*)" is how he'd described the Janus (after the Roman God of Doorways) faces of a single continuum. "One is the outer world of people and objects and the other is the inner world of thoughts and feelings," Swami Shankarananda explains. "Each has its laws and each its forms of education. We have explored the outer world in detail; however we have neglected the inner world." Swamiji calls conventional education as First Education or Knowledge Tradition. The other is Second Education or Wisdom Tradition. This says true happiness lies within. And it can be realized. The process of awakening to Second Education is called inner work. It works on 'being'. It does not give much information in the usual sense, but it empowers us. It turns a weak person into a strong one.

Separate Happiness From Want

Vithal C Nadkarni

SALLY HAWKINS PLAYS Poppy, the irrepressibly cheerful protagonist, in the movie *Happy Go Lucky*. The thirty-year-old primary school teacher, who lives in London with her best friend and flat-mate, is the sort of character who experiences everything around her as a Pollyanna would — in an 'infinitely optimistic and accepting' way. Pollyanna is the heroine of the children's classic by Eleanor Porter. An orphan who lives with a rich autocratic aunt, Pollyanna overcomes her difficulties with the philosophy of 'the Glad Game' originally devised by her late father. This aims at converting every adversity into advantage with sleight of mind.

Pollyanna's Indian counterpart would be the person who greets every event, be it sad, bad or glad, with a jolly 'Jai Ho!' This echoes a happy-go-lucky attitude often associated either with mindless innocence or feeblemindedness. On the plus side, Poppy's never-say-die attitude does seem to insulate her against nasty characters. But on the downside, her relentlessly upbeat attitude also gets her into some scary situations as when she tries to befriend a mentally disturbed homeless man harbouring violent tendencies.

It makes you wonder if it's possible for someone to be too happy-go-lucky for their own good. It also reminds you of Aldus Huxley's *Brave New World* from which unhappiness has supposedly been eliminated. But it still requires unending vigilance: 'Everybody's happy now' is the mantra repeated to the young 150 times a night for the first twelve years of life. Any dissonance that may still survive into adulthood is to be treated with the synthetic drug Soma 'one cubic centimetre of which cures ten gloomy sentiments'.

The only problem, unhappiness still persists. That may be because it's too deeply wired into the human psyche to be banished permanently; negative emotions such a fear and suspicion conferred a survival edge on our ancestors. Happiness also tends to be a fleeting state of mind for a similar reason, explains Daniel Nettle in *Happiness: The Science Behind Your Smile*, which also explains why the urge of wanting something, versus that of liking something, may have been separated for evolutionary reasons. Most people think they like money, status and power when they may just want them. This loses its shine the moment they get what they want. Better to separate happiness from want.

Bliss is Just a Few Breaths Away

Vithal C Nadkarni

BECOME AWARE OF your breath this instant. Go on. How's your breathing? Are you taking deep, smooth breaths, with nice big pauses between inhalation and exhalation? Then you'd have to be a relaxed, chilled-out dude.

But what if you are gasping like a stressed fish pulled out of water? In sharp contrast would be the state of breathing so fine and steady that one's getting by with barely handful of breaths in every minute. That sounds almost like the yogic ideal, where breathing practically stops as the aspirant supposedly gets into a blissful state of super-consciousness called *samadhi*.

In the world according to yoga, the state of your breathing can often be correlated with the state of your mind. Paradoxically, the *Siva-Samhita* also warns that it's futile to measure the heaviness and lightness of inspired and expired air: for that may not necessarily lead one to self-knowledge. But it does tame stress, with what Harvard scientist Herbert Benson dubbed as relaxation response.

The great advantage of this technique is that it requires no special posture or place. You can do it anywhere, anytime. All you have to do is to sit or recline comfortably; close your eyes if you can (obviously not if you are at the wheel) and consciously relax your muscles. Now breathe deeply. To make sure that you are doing it right, keep one of your hands on your tummy and the other on your chest: breathe in slowly through your nose, and as you do so, you should feel your tummy and not the chest rise.

Now exhale slowly. Try to focus on your action as you let out the breath. Adding a meditative element — silently repeating a word (such as 'sa') as you exhale — may help you do better in clearing or refreshing your mind. Conversely, do not get agitated if thoughts intrude. Just don't dwell on them. Allow them pass on and gently return to focusing on your breathing.

Then there's the cleansing breath technique advocated by San Diego psychologist Robert Epstein: Take a huge breath in. Hold it for three to four seconds. Then let it out v-e-r-y s-l-o-w-l-y. As you blow out, blow out all the tension in your body.

The experience of stress in the past magnifies your reactivity to stress in the future. So take a nice deep breath and find a stress-stopping routine this instant. Doing this for 15 to 20 minutes everyday helps you to get into a calmer mode of mind, one that sees you through otherwise stressful situations.

Strive to Live Well, & Fully

Vithal C Nadkarni

COMIC BOOK CHARACTERS like Prince Valiant or Tarzan are much older than Asterix the Gaul. The diminutive warrior's first adventure appeared in a French magazine in 1959. That makes him only fifty; which, even by non-Gallic standards, is still prime-time.

His newest adventure, his 34th, is all set for release and it's expected to sell zillions of copies in 107 languages. So why not party? As they say at the end of each of his adventures, "Bring out the victuals and the mead and carouse away happily, as long as you don't let Cacofonix the Bard to sing!" The problem is, not everyone agrees.

Serious lovers of Asterix series claim the French icon's last album of true merit was Asterix in Belgium. It was also the last album the scriptwriter Rene Goscinny worked on before his death in 1977 with the creator of the cartoon, the Italian-born artist, Albert Uderzo. According to the purists, Asterix hasn't quite been up to his old standard ever since.

Paradoxically, the Asterix albums have never sold as many as they do now. For all its commercial success, some purists would like to 'retire' Brand Asterix. This might entail sending him into the forest-of-no-return, just as they sent once mighty-but-now-aged kings and their preceptors, such as the Druidic Getafixit, into that final state of oblivion called Vanaprastha — it literally means 'entering the forest' in Sanskrit — in the Indian tradition.

Of course, Uderzo will have none of that. "Asterix must live on after me," the artist who is 82, told reporters once. He has already sold the rights to a publishing conglomerate. So does this mark the triumph of mass-marketing, as some critics allege, over artistic merit? Not necessarily.

We must remember art does not have to imitate life. Notice how Lord Greystoke aka Tarzan thumbs his nose at the Grim Reaper with his ageless spouse, Jane Porter. Who knows with infusion of genius and fresh talent Asterix might still get a new life.

Alas, real life dictates otherwise. Notwithstanding claims made by futurists like Raymond Kurzweil, humans simply aren't 'living long enough to live forever'.

One can pop away hundreds of supplements, guzzle gallons of alkaline water and green tea, as Kurzweil reportedly does daily, but that won't 'reprogramme' your biochemistry.

That, however, is not a call to apathy, far less for premature retirement. Strive to live well, fully.

The Luxury on Top of a Cliff

Mukul Sharma

A DEEPLY TROUBLED adolescent eagle returned to its nest one evening and asked his father, "Dad, is it true that we should follow our bliss?" The elder eagle, with years of inexperience behind him, sighed and replied, "Only conscious creatures have the luxury to indulge in such thoughts. We, on the other hand, who have no idea that we're living and neither any notion when death overtakes us, possess more pressing priorities. We follow our hunger. Therefore, go out tomorrow as usual and practice killing field rodents and baby rabbits and, after a few seasons, look for a female eagle. End of story." The mother, who was almost dozing off by then, turned and said, "I don't know why you bother. That kid's goofy in the head."

Years later, after both his parents had dropped out of the sky, the young eagle had become an extremely proficient predator. He could swoop effortlessly down on small furry animals and with his honed claws and beak, rip them to shreds. Also, by this time, he had found a mate who bore him many clutches of mindless eagles who never returned to the nest and asked him anything in the evening except for more space to sleep. But what no one knew was that he still remained deeply troubled. Times when he was really frustrated, he would mutter to himself, "But what if I'm conscious? Would I have the luxury then?"

"Not necessarily," said the Wise One. He was a mythical eagle who lived alone in an old eyrie atop a steep cliff face many flights away from where the others of his kind dwelt and who our young eagle in desperation had one day forsaken his eagle ways to seek out. "Just because your father said something to you once doesn't make it false. Nor does your constant dwelling on it."

"What makes things true then?" queried our hero. "Or, more to the point, should I be following my bliss instead of simply hunting and mating and not knowing if I'm alive or dead?" The Wise One looked away into the horizon in silence and spoke after a long time. "I could have told you," he said, "that hunting and mating was indeed your bliss, but you seemed to have heeded your father a little too literally and followed your hunger. In which case, you now have the rare honour of being the next Wise One atop this lonely but conscious cliff, your only bliss from now on. Happy, goof?" Saying that, he went to the edge of the precipice and dropped out of the sky.

Friendships Make Us Feel Good

Vithal C Nadkarni

ALONG WITH OTHER cast members of *Friends*, Jennifer Aniston became very emotional while filming the final episode of the sit-com. "We are like delicate china right now," she said wiping her tears, "and we are speeding towards a brick wall."

Aniston was speaking about the breaking up of friends rather than of friendships. These were supposed to be stronger; more like Teflon than brittle ceramic. And they endured in episode after episode, despite colliding with bigger brick walls.

Real life is different. Psychologists say most of us would prefer to think that we love our friends because of who they are. Yet studies reveal a curiously narcissistic effect: we tend to bond best with those who support or reinforce our sense of who we are. This insight brought fame and fortune to Dale Carnegie and his *How To Win Friends And Influence People*. Celebrated writer Samuel Johnson offered one more when he said, "A man, Sir, should keep his friendship in constant repair."

Unfortunately our capacity to do so doesn't remain constant itself: psychologists say while our notion of what makes a good friendship varies little as we grow older, our capacity to nurture one does decline. While the spirit may often be willing, the flesh proves poignantly weak! Like everything else in life, if you want to remain friends with someone, you had better be prepared to put in some work, at repairs.

The 'friendly garage' has four walls, psychologist Debra Oswald says. The first two, self-disclosure and supportiveness, are facilitated by communication. Both behaviours are essential for nurturing intimacy of friendship. This not only enhances the quality of life but as latest research shows, lengthens its span too!

We must be willing to extend ourselves, to share our life with our friends, to keep them abreast of what's going on with us. Likewise, we need to listen to them and offer support, Oswald says.

Other studies have shown that physical proximity is no longer an impediment to keeping friendships in repair in our wired world. Still, interaction remains the third essential ingredient in fostering of friendships. "The specific activity doesn't matter," says Oswald. "The important thing is to interact."

The fourth behaviour for having friends, and keeping them, involves being positive. Retain your tact and grace, even under pressure. Ultimately, the best friendships make us feel good.

True Joy Lies Beyond all Money

K Vijayaraghavan

MANY OPINE THAT being successful in life means making lots of money and having significant properties against one's name. There also are many others, who would, instead of becoming 'successful' in this conventional sense, prefer to make a 'success' of their lives, through tangible accomplishments in their chosen fields of activity. This process of striving for excellence, they feel, alone can lend fulfilment and meaning to life, regardless of the materialistic assets which they could boast of. Money, for this category of persons, becomes a means to an end and not an end in itself. Like an arm or leg, money has to be made to do its function and work. Otherwise, it could become a burden.

Though it is difficult to lay down any firm directions for adopting a right approach to this issue, certain broad concepts and guidelines, including particular findings, could be of use for individual application.

A pioneering work was conducted by Talya Miron-Shatz of Woodrow Wilson School and Daniel Kahneman, a Princeton professor. This study (as reported in *The Times of India,* March 19, 2009), reveals that many, who had plenty of money still kept worrying. Instead, those who were not too concerned with savings or making ends meet, reported greater peace. The study noted that happiness did not necessarily increase commensurate with improved financial status.

Besides the concept of 'cutting one's coat according to the cloth available', the crux lies in one's perceptions, approach and attitude towards money. This Cognitive Therapy is thus as applicable to this aspect of life, as to others too. Doubtless, 'security' can finally prove to be as elusive as a mirage!

One powerful message, offering broad hints in this regard, reads: "Money will buy a bed but not sleep; books but not brains; food but not appetite; finery but not beauty; a house but not a home; medicine but not health; luxuries but not culture; amusements but not happiness; religion but not salvation; a passport to everywhere but heaven."

Man, indeed, does not live by bread alone! One who shuts his doors to sublime pastures of this wide and vast world forfeits the possibility of experiencing that unalloyed virtue of true joy. This supreme virtue is termed rightly also as 'happiness', which is not a destination one arrives at but, more so, a means of travelling. This travel guides the aspirant to those innumerable and rewarding islets in what is otherwise a vast, dreary ocean of drab routine and rat race!

Fine-Tuning Self

How does one face up to the challenges of life without being unduly stressed? Or how do you maintain your poise in a trying situation? The articles in this section seek to answer these and other related questions, showing the right path to harmonious living.

In today's world of cut-throat competition almost everyone is geared to excel. But, says *the Bhagavad Gita*, among thousands of people only a handful aim for excellence and among those who do so very few succeed in their objective. What is it that sets apart the achievers from the non-achievers? It is the ability to prioritize things in life and strong will-power.

While elaborating on the virtue of single-mindedness, the author of an article in this section chooses the following quotation from the Bible to emphasize his point: (James -1, 6) 'He that wavereth is like a wave of the sea driven with the wind and tossed.' Juxtaposed with this is another quote which says, (James -1,8) 'A double-minded man is unstable in all his ways.'

This section centres on the theme of self-motivation or self-improvement. While the authors discuss different aspects of it in different ways, in essence they all imply that your success is determined by your ability to fine-tune your own self.

Submerge the Self to Overcome Hurdles

Vithal C Nadkarni

THE PROVERBIAL LEOPARD is stuck with his spots. Even an ebony one can't shake 'em off. You see them when the light shines on the glossy pelt at odd angles. Even if one were to fall into a tub of paint and strut around on the screen as a Pink Panther, beneath the dye lurks an animal that hasn't gotten rid of its spots.

But the statement about the indelible spots isn't so much about leopards as it is about humans. It's about the difficulty of changing what seem like hard-wired personality traits. So what does one make of all those self-help books that tell you otherwise? There is no straight-forward answer.

Some therapists start with the so-called paradox of change; trying to change one's psychology primarily seems to require one's own psychology to initiate and sustain that change. But isn't that like putting the inmates in charge of the asylum, they ask. To make necessary changes in your equipment, you need a software specialist or a therapeutic catalyst.

People of faith advise a different strategy. Their contention is that most of us tend to think only of ourselves as who we are in the present moment: in the current second, 'we' are these anxiously scheming or aching with desire or bursting with disappointment kind of creatures which live from one micro moment to another micro moment. We are mostly unaware of the large context of the ever-present mystery of space and time.

Viewed against the majesty of this metadimension, our lives are but tiny blinks, infinitesimal histories that shine and fade within the larger context of infinite space and time. Of course recognition of that grandeur ought not to trivialize our lives: for despite our seemingly tragic temporal and spatial limitations, we do have a part to play in the larger cosmic scheme or meaning of things.

To be fair, the same effect can be achieved from an atheistic perspective, one that juxtaposes the normal or mundane view of our daily moments with that which takes in the larger frame: the metaview sees us as parts of the universe that are connected to the Whole. That cosmic connection is what supposedly provides us the means to change ourselves. So by tapping into the secondary or unlimited metaidentity we are able to change the immediate or limited or individual aspect of our personality. This is what the Lord advises Arjuna in *the Bhagavad Gita*: submerge your identity to overcome all obstacles.

An Iron Hand — But in a Velvet Glove

K Vijayaraghavan

ON THE IMPORTANCE of being steadfast in one's pursuit and progress, not being wavered by factors within or without, three highly powerful quotes from the Bible are very relevant. While one cautions (Luke - 9, 62) against looking back after putting the 'hand to the plough', the other (James - 1, 6) observes, 'He that wavereth is like a wave of the sea driven with the wind and tossed'. The Book also cautions (James - 1, 8) that always, 'a double-minded man is unstable in all his ways'.

One who boldly scorns temptations, allurements and also pressures from all over is the one who obtains final fulfilment to his quest. The dictates of Vivekananda to 'detach yourself from everything, however much the soul might yearn for it' and that of Ayn Rand to 'live up to your highest vision of yourself no matter what the circumstances you might encounter' — these are guidelines to the earnest aspirant to ensure that his heart does not overpower his head.

In his *The Moon and Sixpence*, Somerset Maugham portrays the character of Charles Strickland who, in his single-minded pursuit, learns not merely to sacrifice his own sinecure living, but also 'to sacrifice others'! The enlightened, though brutal indifference to the shallow, is epitomized by the reply of a highly evolved character, in Ayn Rand's *Fountainhead*, who on a charlatan's asking eagerly, "What do you think of me?" replies casually, "I don't think of you"!

The need for clarity is expressed fully in *the Bhagavad Gita* concepts (2 - 55, 56 and 3 - 17) of *sthira dhee munih* and also *sthithaprajna* meaning, 'the seeker of steadfast mind and one who is stable in wisdom'.

In his pursuit, the true aspirant would always be guided in a manner that he does not ever lose his human qualities, becoming unfeeling or cruel to others just to obtain his objective. Only he, who pursues an unclear or a sinful objective, would cause harm through his obstinacy or selfishness. When clarity reigns and the end is always sublime, prompted by self-knowledge and inner discovery, there would always prevail a strength of character generating that genuinely professional approach, which would also be marked by concern for others around, as long as they too are genuine and worthy.

Such a noble approach may appear, at first sight, to be ruthless. But a closer understanding would reveal the wisdom and sense of precision within. This verily is the practical working of the well-known concept, 'iron hand in a velvet glove'. This also, indeed, is practical wisdom!

Perpetual Peace, & Utopian Myth

Vithal C Nadkarni

AT ANKOR WAT, King Suryavarman II stands forever in a sandstone panel overlooking a gallery. Halfway along that bas relief he's shown again, riding a war elephant with 15 parasols, surrounded by armed columns. Weapons bristle against the flower-printed coats and stylized coiffures of the soldiers. Pointing to the swords and halberds on the wall, the guide draws your attention to the role of weapons in the Cambodia's tragic history. "Remember, the anti-personnel mines and mortars that you saw at the War Museum on the way to the temple in the morning?" he asks. "They are all blood-brothers of the swords and spears used by the Khmer in ancient times."

The crippled war veteran sporting jungle green fatigues at the museum was more taciturn. He said he lost his arm while fighting the murderous Khmer Rouge and his entire family perished in the great wave of terror that Comrade Pol Pot unleashed on this gentle land. He said all this without expression, as though he'd lost all feeling. Upon further probing, he talked softly about his nightmares; about never being able to reach his children in time; about finding them lying bloody and still in a lush green paddy field. What about his fellow citizens who'd had a hand in murdering more than a quarter of Cambodia's population? Had he met any one of them?

For a long time he did not answer. As you waited for him to speak, you could feel the sunshine on your back as grasshoppers leapt among the weeds growing around the rusting relics of war. Then he started speaking about great bewilderment, about an even greater sorrow for being born on this Earth and the few questions that he had for the killers: "Why? What had his kids done to deserve such a fate?" No answer could possibly wipe out his anguish. But he would never stop searching: the Cambodian veteran's endless quest for explanations reminded you of something attributed to Freud: that there could be no 'final solution' to the 'problem of evil'. Freud believed that human life was such that evil impulses 'may be temporarily held in check, suppressed or repressed, but never permanently eliminated'. He recognized that good maxims would not make moral dilemmas go away. In such a scheme, the possibility of perpetual peace was a utopian myth for human life was marked by nothing so much as the transience of beauty and good and evil as well. The great mystery, as the *Bhagavad Gita* says, lay at the beginning and the end of beings; they were manifest only in the middle (*mayadhya-vyaakta*). So we must use it well, or lose it completely!

Live Boldly by Your Chosen Priorities

K Vijayaraghavan

THE BHAGAVAD GITA rightly observes (7, 3) that among thousands, scarcely one strives for excellence and out of those who thus strive, very few attain the ultimate objective.

Why is it that out of the many 'also-ran' cases, very few make it to the finishing line? What is it that differentiates the achiever from those, who, in spite of the burning fire within to rise above the ordinary, finally are left high and dry, reconciled to the mediocre?

Though lack of clarity in priorities and inadequate will power are often cited as the reasons, there lie deep within, other factors too. While some of these are not fully determinable, linked as they are to inscrutable laws of action and effect or destiny (karma or *samskara*), there would emerge clearly a particular factor, which often distinguishes the truly great from others. This is the capacity to be practical, resisting the natural instinct to be needlessly sentimental and attached, reflected often in the feeling that steadfast pursuit of vision could stand in the way of happiness and security of those near and dear. Such feelings inevitably would lead to vacillation and ultimately to surrender to mediocrity, pressure[illegible] also by insinuations and complaints from all over.

The true and steadfast aspirant would, however, [illegible] thus unaffected by such inevitable factors, app[illegible] Horace Walpole: 'This world is a [illegible] tragedy for those that fe[illegible] message of *the Bhagavad Gita* that it is necessary to subdue and if imperative, to eliminate one's own kith and kin, in one's journey to rightful living.

This, verily, is also Vivekananda's exhortation to detach 'from everything, however beloved, however much the soul might yearn for it.....'. These also are Ayn Rand's concept of enlightened selfishness and Patanjali's reference to healthy indifference (*upekshana*) to the sinful (Sutra - 1, 33).

Right and sane living, thus, also demands positive assertiveness — the courage to say 'No' to needless entanglements, commitments or relationships. Not ever caring for what others may say or think, the dynamic seeker practically applies all the precepts on right and effective living (concepts of 'faith and works' and *jnanam, kriya*). Never vacillating, he is enthroned in consistency, a vital element contributing to equanimity (*samatvam*). This, indeed, is that virtue, which, like skill in action (*karmasu kousalam*), is termed by *the Bhagavad Gita* as true yoga!

Be Clear About Your Priorities

K Vijayaraghavan

THROUGH INTELLIGENCE, APPLICATION and a healthy dose of scepticism, the seeker would divine the right types of spiritual practices, meditation, worship and particular religious rituals, which may be needed for his inner purification, leading ultimately to effectiveness. Comprehending that these practices are primarily and merely the means to attain this ultimate objective, he would never get overly occupied with these, thus reducing his dependence on these by and by. Blessed by the right rationalism and pragmatism, he would never ever be affected by blind faith, superstitions or actions motivated by fear of factors within or without. This process also verily is that of being led well in every way, in the spirit of the ancient Indian prayer, *asato ma sat gamaya, tamaso ma jyotir gamaya, mrityo ma amritam gamaya.*

Whatever be the nature of approach, the basis should be that of setting one's priorities clear and sticking to these, to the extent possible, with a resolute commitment. An illustration in this regard concerns a student, who was taking lessons from an Indian yoga teacher, during a course held in America. One day, this eager student came to the class, a few minutes late. Apologizing profusely, she said, "I am sorry, I was held up as I had to make the funeral arrangements for my mother, who suddenly passed away early today". Indeed, this is a typical case study of the power of will against odds!

An incisive article in this regard, 'What makes Olympic Champions' (Reader's Digest, September 1994) also deals with specific cases, where clarity and single-mindedness win for the aspirant the desired results.

Any worthwhile endeavour goes with a price and the needed sacrifices. Conformity, fear, anxiety, insecurity, inadequacy, living by others' priorities, shallow relationships, enforced commitments: these merely militate against one's chosen objectives and vision.

Indeed, the old order should change yielding place to the new, ringing out the old and ringing in the new, guided by the exhortation of Samuel Smiles, 'A place for everything and everything in its place'. This change management confers the eternal rewards of natural time management, precision, control, effectiveness, peace, flow and elegance.

There lies within us all the power of conscious choice, leading to tangible action and ultimately to accomplishment, through boldly living by right priorities. This, essentially and eventually, is the essence of all spirituality too!

Live in the Present, Wisely & Earnestly

Vithal C Nadkarni

DO NOT MOURN the past, says the Buddha. That is the secret of health both for the mind and the body. Nor should you worry about the future, he adds. Instead, one ought to live in the present moment, wisely and earnestly.

Buddha's insight emphasizes a subtle paradox that can only be noticed when you step back from the continuing stream of consciousness.

Of course, we are all living in the present, here and now, you might ask: When else would we be living? Yet a moment's self-reflection would show that many of us live 'everywhere' except in the present moment — we are either fretting over spilt milk or worrying about future milk spills. Either way, one ends up missing out on what the German born mystic Eckhart Tolle in his global blockbuster calls *The Power of Now*. But a sense of the past and the future remains absolutely critical. Without the crucial ability to take that mental step backward or forward away from the perfect present, life becomes a meaningless nightmare without end. Nothing illustrates this better than the poignant case of Henry Molaison (HM), the man without memories, who died in the year 2008 at the age of 82 in America.

HM's life came to a standstill in 1953 when he underwent brain surgery to cure intractable epilepsy. Parts of the brain critical to the formation of new memories were removed from the 27-year-old's brain. He went on to become the world's most unforgettable amnesiac. Although he continued to meet the same doctor day after day for nearly 50 years, each meeting was like a new one for HM. "He never recognized me even if I had been with him the whole day," said the 90-year-old neuropsychologist who used to treat HM. "He was extremely polite. But I could pass him in the waiting room and he wouldn't bat an eyelid."

His IQ wasn't impaired and he had a sharp memory of events before the operation. Nor was his procedural memory lost. HM could perform a complicated task he'd learnt the previous day. But he had no conscious knowledge of having mastered the skill.

This is what put him beyond the pale of 'normal' humanity. For 55 years, he kept waking everyday without knowing where he was. If he looked out the window, he recognized nothing and no one. He was said to be 'a big, mild bear of a man' who 'smiled easily and spoke few words'. He was also polite and always helpful. Thus he could pass as a perfect yogi. But who would ever want to be in such a state of innocence?

Talent Alone Won't Ensure Success

Vithal C Nadkarni

EVERYBODY LOVES THE sweet smell of success. But the stench of failure has few takers. That may explain why those who own up are often derided as masochists or failures. But what if they are smart enough to leverage adversity into advantage? One might then wind up as a case-study in a biz school review, as a central minister allegedly did by vigorously implementing the initiatives of a predecessor.

Whatever the route or modus operandi, talent alone is not enough to ensure success, argues Malcolm Gladwell, the bestselling author of *Tipping Point and Blink,* in his new book, *Outliers.* Opportunity, timing, luck and hard work play their role too.

'No one — not rock stars, not professional athletes, not software billionaires, and not even geniuses — ever makes it alone,' Gladwell adds in his book sub-titled as a *'Story of Success'.*

To be fair, Malcolm does not completely discount individual brilliance and talent. He merely puts it in the context of 'a web of advantages and inheritances'. This is often unacknowledged or underplayed in the 'me-alone' sort of success stories that Horatio Braggarts love to tell.

That apparently applies to the success of Microsoft mogul Bill Gates by his own admission. He was lucky enough to attend a school that, very rarely for any school in those days, had a computer connection to a mainframe. Thus his talent for programming got an early opportunity to flourish.

He also came of age just as personal computers became a reality, and he exploited the opportunity by applying what Gladwell calls the '10,000-hour rule': high achievers need to accumulate that much practice in their formative years if they have to make a mark.

In such a scheme, a protagonist is not a singularly talented person who took advantage of opportunities. He is, instead, a talented person who took advantage of singular opportunities. So how does one spot these 'singular' opportunities? One way is to broaden the field, to make it more inclusive and open for achievement.

Such a prescription is less likely to attract those seeking instant solutions such as the sure-step formula to zero size nirvana, or ten habits of the planet's most successful people (if you can define them). Most of these manuals also bank on hope, which, to quote a Sanskrit proverb, is a strange chain, 'turning those free of it into cripples and those bound into runners in life's rat race'. How else to win it?

Remember, Change is the Only Constant

Vithal C Nadkarni

ONCE UPON A time, there lived a warlord in Japan. He had an only child, a daughter for whom the Shogun would do anything. One day, when it was raining rabbits and foxes, the princess saw rain drops falling like lustrous Mikimoto pearls in her courtyard pond. That's when the fancy struck her to possess a necklace made of rain drops from the pond.

She had only to express her wish and the doting father summoned the best craftsmen from the land. The artists peered carefully at the rain drops falling into the pond and then at each others' faces with growing alarm. For although they tried their best, they just could not skim out the droplets, forget about stringing them. Admission of failure, however, would be tantamount to inviting hara-kiri.

It was in this acute state of embarrassment at the courtyard that the court jester burst forth: "Surely the task shouldn't be so difficult?" he said, venturing boldly where wiser souls shuddered to tread.

"And pray, how do you propose to come up with that matchless necklace for our princess?" the warlord asked contemptuously. "Who can be so bold as to fathom the princess's mind?" the jester parried with great obsequies. "She must therefore make her own selection and hand us over the precious beads of water. The rest ought to be completed in a jiffy," he said with a straight face.

The princess went to the edge of the pond and tried to capture the raindrops without any success. She might as well have tried to fish out the reflection of the moon from the pond as snare a raindrop from it — each one that she touched burst at once.

"Perhaps the Highness has changed her mind?" the joker suggested humbly. "She does not desire the baubles any more?"

Rather than suffer further loss of face, the princess quickly assented: "Yes. I would rather have a nosegay of pretty flowers."

The moral of the Japanese fable is based on the Buddhist Doctrine of Impermanence or *Anitya*: people and events too can be looked upon simply as impersonal products of causes and conditions just like rain drops falling randomly on the pond. We mistakenly attribute intrinsic meanings and significance to them. Everything is in a flux: change is the only constant. Those failing to recognize the fundamental truth are guilty of *abhinivesha* says Patanjali in his *Yoga Sutra*. It is the root of all other *kleshas* and fear lies at its core. It can only be overcome with the most subtle practice.

Attitude May Matter More Than Talent

Vithal C Nadkarni

MUSIC COMPOSER ELLIOT Carter celebrated his 100th birthday in December 2008 with a concert at Carnegie Hall. It featured a 17-minute piece for piano and orchestra that Carter wrote when he was 98. Talk about thumbing your nose at mortality! Carter has already lived three times as long as Schubert and 65 years more than Mozart. Yet his first opera premiered in 1999 and he produced seven works in 2007 and six more this year.

Since he turned 90, the composer who many critics rank among the greatest ever, has churned out more than 40 pieces and he shows no signs of slowing down. Aficionados say he's still writing at the top of his form and every piece has new ideas that he's trying out along with subtle refinements of those presented earlier.

However, not everybody in the audience takes easily to his works which are sometimes described as 'complicated'. Carter, who has a penchant for contemporary compositions rather than old music, remains unruffled. While he attributes his success to 'just a matter of luck', he also adds impishly, "Once society gets more complicated, people will have to become much cleverer and much sharper. Then they will like my music."

Carter is, of course, alluding to the so-called Flynn Effect (named after psychologist James R Flynn) and the social multiplier phenomenon, which has documented a spectacular rise in IQ measurement over the generations (which simply means environmental factors can influence the average IQ of a population).

At an individual level, Carter's life offers a heroic example of unwavering faith married to unstinting effort. This can be particularly inspiring to younger contenders who fear loss of heart and burn-out. If he can be that productive at 100, just imagine how much you could do even if you make a fresh start at half or quarter of his age. Their effort, however needs to be backed by what creativity wonks like Colin Martindale called 'Cognitive Disinhibition', which refers to the ability to focus or defocus attention as per task demands. So one 'first learns the rules and then breaks 'em!'

It also shows that for genius to thrive, at any age, attitude may be even more important than talent. This entails what the investment guru Warren Buffet called 'the art of not getting in your own way'. "It's not about your potential horse power," Mr Buffet told a PBS programme. 'Whatever you have, learn to utilize it fully'; till the very end.

Just a Thinking Person's Reality

Mukul Sharma

THE FACT THAT most times we only perceive what we can conceive is dramatically borne out by what happened to Captain Cook when his ship reached the island of Tahiti in 1769. The Tahitians couldn't see the vessel even though it was moored directly in front of them. The reason a big sea-going craft like that was invisible to them was because they couldn't visualize such a structure, having had no previous exposure to something like it in all their experience, history, myths or imagination. As a result there was no modelling system available which could reconstruct its image with any meaningful correspondence to reality.

Even up to 70 years later, by which time a lot of missionary and other European ships had come into contact with the islanders, they still could only manage to describe ships as floating islands inhabited by beings of a superior nature, upon whose orders lightning flashed and thunder rumbled (the muskets and cannons on board). Today, a local Tahitian tourist guide can tell the engine difference between two brands of water scooters.

The philosopher Alfred North Whitehead also drew attention to this by saying that our conditioned mode of thinking and use of language affects our view of reality to such a great extent that it becomes virtually impossible for us to fully appreciate its magnitude. There are some fundamental assumptions, he said, which we unconsciously presuppose and these appear so obvious that people don't know what they are assuming because no other way of putting things has ever occurred to them. In other words, we can't really contemplate what we have no comprehension of, even if it is right in front of us. Therefore, the range of our knowledge of reality is limited by our preexisting beliefs and expectations.

Of course, having a consensus world view is a convenience since it's practical and has survival value. Nevertheless, it can be dangerous to forget that it's also a convenient fiction because when there's no new expectation, nothing new gets to happen and the 'out there' becomes falsely fixed. At the same time, the world that a bat or a shark sees is not the same as what we do and we blithely regard their interpretation of it as seriously flawed even though they survive by means of it just like we do with ours. Who's correct? As the physicist James Jeans put it: "The universe begins to look more like a great thought than a great machine."

Real Benefits from Great Writings

K Vijayaraghavan

DOUBTLESS, THERE EXISTS, in this great world, in abundant measure, great and inspiring writings besides specific injunctions on worthwhile living. The question however arises: "Are these truly and practically applicable?" The answer to this is yes or no, depending on how these are put to use and applied.

When such resources are read merely for titillating the intellect or plain entertainment, the result could, at best, be a temporary motivation. Sooner or later, the person concerned could slip back, thereby limiting the scope of these resources to mere theory or just pleasant literature.

However, when the seeking aspirant, after identifying those pieces of writings or exposures, which would suit him best, integrates these in his personality, these could transform his very nature. He would thus obtain immense practical benefits, both within and without. By harmonizing the different aspects within and thus being 'in touch' with his real self, he commences to touch the lives of others too, radiating clarity, cheer and warmth all over, obtaining also for himself effectiveness, harmony and clarity in his priorities.

The question now arises on the actual means to be adopted for realizing this objective. The process begins with cultivating reverence for the goal set for oneself and also for these sublime concepts and writings. Studiously pondering over these, in the stillness of the wish power within (that 'state of least disturbance'), would ensure that these take firm roots to flower forth for the benefit of the person concerned and others too, as militating and conflicting aspects within are resolved by and by. This also is the process of knowledge being translated into experience, in line with the Biblical concept of 'faith and works'.

In fact, inspiring writings and great books assume newer and greater dimensions, especially when these are savoured more than once. Another means to bring about positive changes is through merely dwelling on and pondering over subtle messages of wisdom and truth and one's own observations and experiences in life. Exchanging ideas and discussions in the earnest company of those, who too are spurred with that urge for creative and effective living (***satsang***), is also a powerful aid in this regard.

Limitless, therefore, is the potential for harnessing the power inherent in creative writings and nature's own promptings. These indeed abound all over for the benefit of the aspiring individual!

Mainly on Closure & Moving on

Mukul Sharma

A CLOSE FRIEND'S father died a couple of days back. At the same time there was a party planned by another common friend. Second friend was now in a fix. Should she go through with it? Like, was it too close to the grief? Would it appear insensitive? Should it be brought up at all? Anyway, in the end, a vague kind of 'common sense' prevailed and it was consensually decided that perhaps everyone could get together after a few days or weeks had passed and the bereaved had attained some sort of closure.

Now, there's a word we need to get a good handle on these days as far as terminal loss is concerned. Closure. Earlier this used to be a largely passive, automatic and understood process. Some loved one died or left us heart-dead and it took us — what? — a few weeks, months or even years maybe before we got back into the stride of everyday life again. The system worked for thousands of years because it had to if people had to do what they had to in order to carry on existing. It was a way of easing back, largely unnoticed, into the world of, well, partying for instance. An analogue experience if you will.

Of late, however, it's been digitized and made proactive. For instance, we read or hear of people saying that catching and convicting the person responsible for a murder will provide both the victim and those left living, with closure. Then, it's been defined:

closure is the state of experiencing an emotional conclusion to a difficult life event. After that, it's been scaled. A person with a high need for closure prefers order and predictability and is decisive and close-minded. He or she also feels discomfort with ambiguity. Someone rating low on need for closure expresses more ideational fluidity and emits more creative acts. Finally, it's been assigned a time frame — not so much in terms of discrete units but as something that has to definitely lead up to 'moving on' as the fixed end point of grieving.

In the light of such complexity, perhaps it might be a good idea if we could start having our collective closures as soon as some loved person was born. For one thing it would give everyone around almost a lifetime to get prepared. Also, since we love ourselves the most, it might be an even better idea to initiate the process of closure on our own lives from the moment we understand the concept of death — say, at some adolescent rite of passage. After all, we're the only ones who will actually be moving on.

A Little Knowledge Goes a Long Way

Mukul Sharma

ONCE UPON A time there was a high IQ cheetah who couldn't run at a top speed of 120km per hour. As a result, the Thompson's gazelles that he chose to chase easily outran him and he was never able to get hold of one. Thus, in order to survive, he was forced to catch rodents and frogs and other small animals which lived in the Serengeti.

Of course he had to do this surreptitiously because if any of the other cheetahs ever found out it would be terribly humiliating for him. "What's the use of being the fastest land animal in the world," he would often say to himself, "if I can't even run down a decent high speed deer for dinner?"

So one day he went to a cheetah who was renowned for her astonishing speed and blurted out his predicament. "I have all the evolutionary adaptations that enable our species to run as fast as we do, including large nostrils that allow for increased oxygen intake, and an enlarged heart and lungs which work together to circulate oxygen efficiently. Also, during a typical chase when I can accelerate from zero to hundred in three seconds my respiratory rate increases from 60 to 150 breaths per minute."

"And, while running, in addition to having good traction due to my semi-retractable claws, I use the tail as a rudder for steering which allows me to make razor sharp turns, necessary to outflank prey who often make such turns. And yet", he concluded lamely, "I can't manage a top speed of 120km an hour no matter how hard I try."

"That's interesting," said the other cheetah who was staring at him wide-eyed by now. "Because you know, all this time I thought my nostrils were for only for smelling and my heart and lungs for keeping me alive. During a chase all I ever had time to notice was that the surroundings became a blur, my breathing increasingly deep and heavy, and by the time it's over I'm pooped for the rest of the day. As for my claws and tail, I just try to keep them clean. But, like I said, this is amazing stuff. If we were to live together I could do the hunting while you can teach me things about myself and the world so that I too can become as knowledgeable as you."

So the two hitched up and soon the Serengeti had two cheetahs that couldn't run at a top speed of 120km an hour and had to live off rats and frogs instead of gazelles to the end of their days.

Moral: A lot of knowledge is also a dangerous thing.

Flow with the Present Moment

Vithal C Nadkarni

LIVING IN THE present is among the remedies recommended to those traumatized by Mumbai's 26/11. It sounds promising but how does one get into that elusive state? How something so simple can be so hard, asks a workshop participant. In response, the guide presents a map of self-created blockages presented by Dr Jay Winner, the founder of the stress reduction programme at Sansum Clinic and author of *Take The Stress Out of Your Life:* The first road block involves 'should and ought' kind of normative thinking: Living in the present involves a profound paradox, says Dr Winner, you cannot pursue it for its benefits. Although our most joyful experiences come out of the times when we are fully present, trying to make a moment have this quality can have the opposite effect.

So if you think the moment should be more joyous, spiritual, or ought to be relaxing, those very qualities might elude you. We can change the future, but the present moment can only be as it is. To be fully mindful therefore you have to give up your goal of how this moment should be better. This is similar to the advice given by the Lord to Arjuna in *the Bhagavad Gita*: concentrate fully on the ongoing action instead of worrying or fantasizing about the quality or impact of its result.

The second great roadblock involves creation of a false attribution: You are not your thoughts! Of course thoughts are incredibly useful, Dr Winner concedes. How could we ever live in today's society if we couldn't think and analyse? However, we must also remember that many thoughts are repetitive judgements about our lives. The trick of circumventing such thoughts lies in using what Vedanta calls witness mode or *sakshi bhava*.

Notice how the barrage begins the first thing in the morning: "I wish I didn't have to wake up yet." "If only the kids would behave." "I can't believe this traffic!" Left unchecked, that stream of thoughts increases stress and frustration, warns Dr Winner. Learn to 'decentre', to realize that you can watch your thoughts and don't have to believe them, he adds.

When you notice a thought wishing the present moment were different, take a figurative step back and realize it is just a thought; you don't have to believe it. But don't resist it too hard either. Just watch. Be aware. Flow with the present moment 'like a breeze that gently ruffles blossoms,' says 13th century poet Mukundaraja, 'without ever getting caught'.

Be Honest, be Also Resourceful

K Vijayaraghavan

MANY WHO CLAIM themselves to be 'practical', feel that to go ahead in life, it is often necessary to compromise on one's integrity. They also point out to many simple and honest persons suffering, especially financially, while those who have been corrupt appear to thrive.

Such philosophy would, prima facie, in fact, appear to hold some water, especially because there also exist many 'honest' persons, who, on observing others' comfortable living, nurse doubts about their own values. They even conclude that one cannot be honest and also be above want at the same time — that is, one cannot have the cake and eat it too!

A deeper analysis would, however, convince that those who take such a cynical view are not simple persons but mere simpletons, whose list of virtues commences with honesty and also ends there. Such 'honest' persons do not have the urge to extend honesty to other needed virtues, so necessary for true fulfilment. Life, limited in this manner, is prosaic, laughable and is, actually, no life at all!

Honesty, inspired by true courage of conviction, would always also go with intelligent hard work, enterprise and dynamism. Thus the seeker not merely obtains peace of an honest mind but also materialistic gains (*artha*), to fulfil his true desires (*kama*). Established in righteousness (dharma), he finally wins liberation (*moksha*) from all wrong living and worldly bondage.

It is through this holistic and integrated approach, 'tireless striving stretches its arms towards perfection'. Its practical working is illustrated by Richard Bach's *Jonathan Livingston Seagull*. Striving for excellence in flight, Jonathan learns to 'find the rare and tasty fish that schooled ten feet below the surface of the ocean' and to 'ride the high winds far inland to dine there on delicate insects'. He is thus the winner, even from the materialistic point of view, having also fulfilled the call of the spirit within.

The late Gomathy Krishnanand, the first principal of Kendriya Vidyalaya, Trivandrum used to inspire her students, telling, 'there is always room at the top' in this vast world, for him, who is good, honest and also willing, daring and resourceful. This awesome combination of such abiding integrity within and also effective persistence would obtain the twin blessings of being both honest and also being prosperous in every way — the blessing of having the cake and eating it too! This, doubtless, is unmatched skill in action (*karmasu kaushalam*)!

Prayers Addressed to Oneself

Mukul Sharma

IN JOSEPH HELLER'S *Catch-22*, an imbecilic army colonel inquires of his chaplain if the man has any prayer which is humorous and doesn't involve things like waters and valleys and God because, as he puts, he would like to stay away from the subject of religion altogether if he could. The chaplain who's terrified of his superior answers somewhat apologetically, "I'm sorry, sir, but just about all the prayers I know are rather sombre in tone and make at least some passing reference to God." As one critic has said, one can find here an indictment of a culture's shallow and ultimately atheistic invocation of God for that culture's own means and ends.

But does that mean atheists can't pray? Or that do such prayers even help? Take *Evan Almighty*, the 2007 environmental comedy film in which Morgan Freeman who plays God tells Evan that when you pray for courage God doesn't give you courage. Instead, He gives you an opportunity to be courageous. Similarly, when you ask for strength, conviction or resolve, He doesn't shower you with those sterling qualities immediately but gives you the opportunity to be strong, convinced or resolved. However, the question that arises here is, does the founding of an opportunity require the intervention of something divine?

Not necessarily. People who need a favourable circumstance to create the potential to acquire an objective don't succeed as well as they would with a sudden bounty of it than if they had fashioned it themselves. Just like it's pretty ridiculous to imagine a person being abruptly over-gifted with the exact quality he or she lacks (which is why Freeman's God doesn't deliver at one go on request but lets it develop on its own). The version of superman as delineated in comics or envisioned by Bernard Shaw and Nietzsche is a goal for humanity to be set for itself from within.

In other words if you think you're in control — as most of us tend to believe we are — then we could give ourselves the opportunity to be the kind of person we want to be by perhaps praying to ourselves. Atheists, of course, wouldn't have any problem with this but so shouldn't those who believe that either a godhead resides in us or that we are indeed manifestations of it. In any case, if there's at least one way in which a prayer does help it's in giving us a chance to answer it ourselves without unnecessarily invoking God. And, with that, comes greater responsibility.

Helping Others will Boost Immunity

Vithal C Nadkarni

WHEN STUDS TERKEL, the renowned author and radio host, died in Chicago in October 2008 at the age of 96, he had a copy of his newest book by his bedside. The book offers a postscript to thoughts from a lifetime of listening by the Pulitzer-winning writer, often called 'Guerrilla journalist' armed a tape recorder that turned voices of ordinary Americans into riveting oral history. He also used to boast that only one other man had 'used the tape recorder with as much fervour as I — Richard Nixon!'

This was his way of battling the collective amnesia, which he described as 'a national Alzheimer's disease', that affects even the most highly documented cultures. Echoing Rene Descartes' famous dictum, Terkel used to quip, 'I tape therefore I am'. But the man who turned ordinary folks who otherwise were mere statistics into real humans with his interviews was unusually reticent about his own feelings and experiences. "It's almost like there's no room inside me to be interested in my own feelings and thoughts," he told an interviewer."

This inner claustrophobia may have been the result of an unhappy childhood. His father was an invalid who suffered from heart disease. His mother was given to unpredictable rages that kept the household on edge. "What nobody got from her was warmth and love, or at least not a display of it," Terkel said. But he got on with his life with characteristic brio, engaging with people at large in a prodigiously creative manner. "I don't have to stay curious, I am curious, about all of it, all the time," he once said. "Curiosity never killed this cat' — that's what I'd like as my epitaph."

That may also reveal the secret of Terkel's remarkably creative longevity. Recent research on elderly people has shown that those who contributed most enthusiastically to their social network showed fewer of the effects of ageing. The more they gave, the more they benefited. Now why should this be so?

One hypothesis is that when we help others we take our minds off ourselves. For nothing deepens depression like dwelling on it. There is also massive evidence to show that helping others boosts the immune system. An oft-cited Harvard study showed that even watching a film of others — nuns in Kolkata working with the poor and dying, for example — boosts your antibodies. So? To live long, focus your curiosity outwards rather than inwards.

Consistency — Basis For all Virtues

K Vijayaraghavan

A BROAD GUIDELINE in forming a set of virtues, as applicable to each, has been set out by sage Patanjali (Sutra - 1, 33). He exhorts the aspirant to develop particular approaches to the four different issues, which concern life-friendly inclination to truly joy-inducing matters, compassion to the sufferings around, delight towards the sublime and indifference to the sinful and the dross. In fact, this apathy to those issues, which do not contribute to one's chosen objectives in life, would by itself aid in nourishing those first three virtues, named by Patanjali. In this process, the retarding forces would drop off, as if naturally.

Whatever be the guideline or signposts chosen to evolve a set of virtues, depending upon one's own personality and attendant circumstances, the seeker of excellence has to ensure consistency and steadiness, guarding against fickleness or waxing and waning and the highs and lows of one's own moods, opinions and perceptions. This also ensures evolving right priorities, clarity and development of one's true interests in life (*swadharma*).

Discarding the needless, and naturally making the needed sacrifices in this single-minded pursuit is the unfolding of the virtue of true and lasting *vairagya*, which defies distractions, temptations and time.

Illustrating this concept, late Sita Venkatachary, a scholar then based at Chennai, often used to refer to three types of superficial *vairagya*. The first, *smasana vairagya*, refers to the ephemeral and new found 'wisdom', felt by him, who on observing, in a funeral, how death is the ultimate reality, is overcome, for just a moment, by a desire to abandon all mundane pursuits. Similar is also the short-lived *purana vairagya*, arising out of listening to the wisdom contained in scriptures. *Prasava vairagya* is on the fleeting philosophical streaks, which grip the woman, suffering the pangs of child birth. Perhaps applicable only to those times, when birth control techniques were unknown, this woman, gripped by a temporary *vairagya*, 'decides' never again to engage in conjugal relationships, lest she should again become pregnant!

In contrast, true and lasting *vairagya*, unlike the above three, would be marked by consistency, courage of conviction and power of resilience and inner strength. This, indeed, obtains for the aspirant, what Benjamin Franklin refers to as 'sacred, substantial, never fading bliss' (emphasis added)!

Right Approach Obtains Fulfilment

K Vijayaraghavan

POSSIBLY ON ACCOUNT of right experiences and exposures (*samskara*) through the passage of their soul over the years, resulting invariably in neutralization of all stressful impacts upon the mind-body mechanism, there could be some, who would never ever need any physical, mental or spiritual exercises. But for most humans, a right combination of these becomes necessary if they are to rise above vegetating levels of drab existence.

Various proven techniques are available in the above regard. The system involving the first four stages of *ashtanga yoga* is just one. Kalaripayattu (the martial art of Kerala), aerobic and isometric workouts, waltz, tango, judo, karate, jogging or long walks — these are also highly effective, depending upon individual nature and needs.

The aspirant has to choose that technique or system, which through his own observation, analysis and application, he would divine, is best suited to his particular personality. The basic prerequisites are that the technique chosen should be joyful and relaxing during and also after the performance, bringing about balanced and holistic development of all parts and functions, not merely empowering one at the expense of the other.

Rooted in awareness and the consequent enthusiasm of looking forward to every subsequent practice, this *sadhana* would generate that fulfilment, which would also serve to free the performer from self-centredness, anxieties, scheming and doubts, enabling him to 'love everybody and everything', to use the expression of Norman Vincent Peale. Blessed also with virtues of resilience and good humour, he would thus translate into practice the spirit of Shakespeare's observation (Hamlet - II, 2): 'There is nothing either good or bad but thinking makes it so'.

Feeling thus always light and freed of those deadweights of unhealthy thoughts and feelings and also those shallow relationships and pursuits, the yearning spirit obtains the needed 'space' for worthwhile, cherished and long sought after virtues and powers to enter, take root and blossom. This also is flying off into one's rightful world of excellence, validating the observation that angels fly because they take themselves lightly.

The entire process is often set in motion by the initial step of choosing the right work out and system of exercises. It is from the regular performance of the practices attendant on the technique thus chosen that blessings and benefits commence to flow naturally!

See Perfection in Others First

Vithal C Nadkarni

AS OUR CAR moves over the Vashi bridge the landscape architect talks about the role played by first impressions in choice and creativity. Her imagination was stirred by an author named Read Montague. His first name sounds like a verb, she thought when she first saw the American neuroscientist's book at a bookstall in downtown Mumbai.

The title *Why Choose This Book?* was as intriguing. Montague, who is currently a fellow at the Institute for Advanced Studies in Princeton, was tracking that slipperiest of beasts called choice. "The sneaky secret about choice is that it's not about choice at all — it's about value," said the neuroscientist who directs an imaging lab at the Baylor College of Medicine. So could he 'explain' why someone roots for a Dark Venus such as Serena Williams while another pines for a blonde goddess called Maria Sharapova?

The act of choosing one action (or actor) over another follows directly from the way the brain values both the external world and the internal world — our thoughts, Montague elaborated. We need valuation because life is short and Time or Art are long! From such humble beginnings, life discovered subtle mechanisms of efficient valuation and embedded them in the human brain, he adds.

"The same mechanisms also constrain our choices and anchor them to our biological needs. Yet they also confer on us the freedom to choose, even to the point of denying our instincts for survival.

What other species can and will die for an idea — even an idea read about in a book?" he asks rhetorically.

Dr Montague's epiphany (as reported by his artistic fan) draws forth a quote in Punjabi from the restaurateur sitting in the back seat of the car. Ghazal maestro Jagjit Singh gave him the lyric composed by the Sufi Shaikh Ghulam Farid at the restaurant: "When someone calls Laila the love of Majnu's life, dark, Majnu says, the caller does not have the discerning eye (*teri ankh na vekhanwali*)," the hotelier declaims. "The Vedas are white and so is the Quran, he goes on. But it's the inky black that puts words of wisdom on white parchment. The Sufi master too has eyes for Him who is beyond dark and light." The moral? 'Don't be swayed by superficialities'. As self-help guru Wayne Dyer says in his *Power of Intention,* if you're unable to see and honour that same perfection in others, it's impossible to know your own perfection. See yourself in all of humanity.

When Standing Up is Not an Option

Mukul Sharma

HE'S A MOTIVATIONAL speaker and, like thousands of his kind, he goes from place to place along the length and breadth of the country he was born in and lectures focusing on the topics that today's people face. He regularly travels internationally too to speak to religious congregations, schools, colleges and corporate bodies. So far, he's spoken to over two million people in 12 countries on four continents. One of his standard lines of patter goes something like this: "Along the way you might fall down. So what do you do when you fall down? Get back up because everybody knows how to get back up. But there are some times in life when you fall down and you feel you don't have the strength to get back up. Do you think you have any hope left then? If I try a hundred times to get back up and I fail a hundred times and give up, do you think I will ever be able to get up? No. But what if I fail and try again? And again, and again, and again? I just want you to know that it's not the end. It matters how you're going to finish. Are you going to finish strong? That's when you'll find that strength to get back up."

Then, as if to drive the point home as dramatically as possible, he deliberately falls down full on his stomach onstage. The audience gasps because Nick Vujicic, who was born with the extremely rare tetra amelia syndrome, a disorder which is characterized by the absence of all four limbs, has no arms or legs at all. And as they see his stump of a body — just a truncated little torso really — topple forward face down, the tired clichés the cheery man's been expounding so long suddenly take on a whole new meaning. Yet the first thing that races through their minds is how's he going to get back up?

As the first of our cave dwelling ancestors quickly discovered out when they began making spears to use on hunts, arms and legs are not only parts of the body but also extensions of the head. Like the tail dropped by a lizard which can only wiggle by itself for a while before becoming inert, left to themselves our limbs can achieve nothing either.

Nick positions his forehead on the floor and uses it to curve the spine inwards to its maximum and then leverages his body back into an upright position. So can he comb and clean and feed himself too? Chances are he can't. But then how many of us who can, end up finishing strong like him?

Tell the Truth If You Want Help

Vithal C Nadkarni

THE 'LAST LECTURE' series at Carnegie Mellon University has a quixotic tradition. Distil a lifetime's wisdom in a single lecture in the event of your being near death. The brief fit Randy Pausch's case chillingly well. The 47-year-old professor of computer science had just been diagnosed with pancreatic cancer. His doctors said he had only three to six months to live. The professor, who had three small kids and a doting wife, took up the gauntlet and delivered a jaw-droppingly inspirational lecture on 'How to really achieve your childhood dreams'.

A newspaper columnist who drove 300miles to attend said, "It was like watching Babe Ruth hit his last home run, or Michael Jordan hitting his jump shot at the end of the NBA finals. It was electric in there. I knew it affected everyone that was there. But I could not have foreseen what followed, even in my wildest dreams."

The journo wrote about the talk and put up excerpts on a website, starting the viral run that ended up with zillions of viewers watching the full speech on the World Wide Web in several avatars. In an age filled with questionable or cheesy self-help tomes, Pausch's straight-from-the-soul swansong was expected to top bestseller charts: his life lessons had already been translated in 18 languages. So what were his childhood dreams? "You may not agree with this list, but I was there. Being in zero gravity; playing in the National Football League; authoring an article in the *World*

Book Encyclopedia. I guess you can tell the nerds early," he said in the lecture.

Although he achieved most of his dreams, Pausch flashed his rejection slips onscreen and spoke about career setbacks: "Brick walls are there for a reason. The brick walls aren't there to keep us out. They are there to show us how badly we want things... Don't complain. Just work harder," he added showing a slide of Jackie Robinson, the first black major league baseball player.

"It was in Robinson's contract not to complain, even when fans spit on him."

How do you get people to help you? "By telling the truth: by being earnest. I'll take an earnest person over a hip person everyday, because hip is short-term," Pausch says.

His paean to truth vibes with a similar trip Nachiketas made to the House of Death in Kathopanishad. His message was rousing: Get up! Stir yourself! Master your fear and attain all-pervading bliss. A hard path, the sages say, sharp as a razor.

Transcendental Thoughts

The section 'Transcendental Thoughts' takes you through a spiritual journey — beyond the realm of the ordinary day-to-day living.

Every common man's lifetime is spent in fulfilling his basic needs and performing his duties. For that he/she tends to employ methods which are sometimes unfair. It is when we are running after our requirements that we tend to run away from ourselves — from our inner being. When one gets distanced from his/her inner self, a nihilistic perspective creeps in his/her mind.

The different articles that appear in this section take us through the personal experiences and anecdotes of immortals and give a peek into what transcendental living or thought is.

According to Dr Andrew Newberg, co-founder of Penn's Centre for Spirituality and the Mind, regular meditation does cause permanent changes in the mind, which in turn leads to a right attitude which liberates you from fears and insecurities. Such a mind has the ability to detach itself, thereby opening the path to perfection. Such a mind is capable of a 'transcendental experience'.

Swami Chidananda Saraswati once said that it was 'a rare blessedness and a great good to enter into spiritual life. And to take it seriously and engage in active spiritual *sadhana* was a second blessedness and a still greater good. But to persevere and to be ever-progressive and ceaseless in one's spiritual life was the greatest good, the crowning blessedness'.

Surviving the Soul Isn't Easy

Mukul Sharma

HAVING AN IMMORTAL soul is a very important and integral part of Christian theology. But it comes with a heavy scientific price — especially as science advances our knowledge of human lineage and evolution. For instance, it was easy at one time for doctrinal apologists to answer the question as to who was the first person to have a soul. All they had to say was: Adam. Unfortunately, that answer doesn't work any longer since only a handful of ultra fundamentalists today attempt to retain the rather simplistic mythology of Genesis. Even the papacy acknowledges the evidence of Darwinism as pretty well established and that humankind goes back millions of years in its making from protohominids to homo sapiens.

However, that doesn't solve the problem either. For if we are to grant that humans possess an eternal soul, there must have been a first-case scenario before which no humans had one. When did such an infusion take place that determined who was mortal and condemned to dust and who were to enjoy or suffer everlasting bliss or damnation? Any god, it seems, would have to be fairly arbitrary in deciding at exactly what point along the continuum of a slowly evolving human species, he, she or it should make the soul come into the picture. And if indeed there was such a precise transition point, one would have to accept that some particular child then existed who had a soul while its parents didn't.

To say that all protohumans, irrespective of their candidature for sapiency, were infused with souls right from the beginning only pushes the question further back. Would the shrew-like creatures from which monkeys and humans descended even understand the import of having a soul or be able to deal with its moral implications? And why deny modern monkeys a soul in that case? Incidentally, if only resurrection is considered instead of a continuously existing immortal soul, then who in the sequence of ancestors leading out from the first to the present will be the first whose body shall be resurrected?

No, the concept of having an immortal soul reserved for only a select few inside a broader range of individuals just doesn't work unless every living organism including bacteria and moss are also considered. And even then viruses are between animate and inanimate. So why leave out rocks and minerals? Funnily enough, there are some religions that actually say everything has a soul. Maybe we could go with them.

On Never Having to Travel at All

Mukul Sharma

HOW FAR DOES one have to travel to say sorry? When hot-headed Huan Tsin was a young novitiate he thought he had once offended his teacher by calling him an unenlightened buffoon who had no right to teach. He had left the monastery at once and gone on to live his life the way he reckoned most others of the world do. Over the years, however, his remorse grew inside him till a day came some ten years later when he left his wife and family and travelled five hundred miles back to the monastery. He knelt humbly before the old master and said he was sorry for what he had done and begged for forgiveness.

A lot of us also need to make similar journeys in order to right old wrongs but the immediate business of life keeps us too busy to undertake them. So everyday appears more and more like no wrong was ever done — especially not by us — and, thus, the thin layer of forgetfulness hardens into a thick skin that memory cannot penetrate any more. After that, even infrequent introspection and honesty is not able to break through such a convenient and comfortable shield.

And, all along, the further and further we move away to other cities and down the years from the once and original hurt we had caused, we fail to realize the journey is just getting longer by the day. But now, how far does one have to travel to accept an apology? This is a far less arduous expedition because it can be accomplished instantly or never at all. Either way, though, it requires hardly any extra courage to carry it off since one is always under the impression one had nothing to do with its perpetration or continuity.

And the travel time is, in fact, measured only in the waiting. We who think we've gone out of our way to forgive someone should actually be wondering about all the time that's been exhausted for it to happen — no matter how redeemed we appear to be feeling afterwards.

Huan Tsin's teacher, on the other hand, was astounded. He said he couldn't understand why the pupil was sorry since he himself hadn't been offended at all and if Huan had understood that in the first place he wouldn't have wasted such a lot of time and space to move his life away from where it had been. So, finally, we have to ask ourselves how far had the teacher travelled? He hadn't moved at all. Or if he had, he had moved a few mountains in the process.

Knowing the Place for the Second Time

Mukul Sharma

THOSE WHO ARE not content with being where they are, or having learnt what they were compulsorily taught to understand, or even too comfortably happy inside their hearts, move on. They move out of their constrained spaces to look around a little bit more and explore. Does it matter to the world at large that they do? Not necessarily. Does it make a difference to it when they have done? Perhaps.

Some travel to places they've never seen, if only to seek what might have been if they had not arisen and resided in just one land or location all their lives. Other mountains and plains, rivers and rains, fascinate them. Over millennia we've come to know them as wanderers, adventurers, journeymen, minstrels, seafarers, Sufis and, yes, sometimes pirates too. New lands have often been unearthed because of them, along with new peoples, new cultures, creeds, lores and mores. Some of them retread their old routes and return from there; some grow older roots to remain elsewhere.

Other people move out of their otherwise safe and guaranteed mental spaces to wander in the mind. Tired of scripts and teachings, they travel in the realms of thought and ideas, taking those paths not taken earlier and discover fresh visions in the arts and sciences of human endeavour which enlighten the rest of us till newer travellers who follow them come up with novel imagery of their own. Thus, instead of beating the same path around similar bushes, the creative knowledge of our humanity keeps advancing and we begin to comprehend more and more of what lies beyond the end of our usual notions.

Yet others adventure out from the soul. Often the thin line between a fine madness and the momentous gets blurred but, in the end — at least unto themselves — such people gain considerably in spirit than what they lose in commodity or kind because they know they've found more in their essence than in the mind. Some indeed combine all kinds of exploration — the physical, mental and spiritual — as did Peter Matthiessen, for instance, in his book *The Snow Leopard* which by no means can simply be called an account of his two-month journey in 1973 to Crystal Mountain in the Dolpo region on the Tibetan Plateau in the Himalayas. It's a travelogue that journeys in and out of all earths. As T S Eliot once wrote:

"...the end of our exploring,
Will be to arrive where we started,
And know the place for the first time."

Be Spiritual, But with a Purpose

K Vijayaraghavan

DOUBTLESS, PRACTICE OF honesty attains fulfilment only when accompanied by other needed virtues of head and heart, calling for enterprise, foresight, dynamism and hard work. Rightly was it noted by a major organization's senior officer, himself upright and dynamic, that he would rather be served by intelligent and resourceful persons, who may otherwise be prone to some minor corruption, than be served by honest dullards!

Indeed, there abound many, who, secretly doubting their own value systems, damage themselves and others, gloating on their 'honesty', incapable of extending this virtue to its logical completion. Similarly, there also exist innumerable 'spiritual' persons whose only claim to this virtue is the vast time spent on stereotyped worship, visit to holy places and 'meditation'. Some even imagine that they are potential messiahs, leading erring humanity to salvation!

An insight would reveal that, more often than not, such persons would be ineffective, incapable of performing even small necessary acts with the needed clarity and briskness. Their single track mind also shuts their eyes to many, who, without depending on any such 'spiritual' exercises, are far more brisk, efficient and creative.

An analysis of the related issues would enable the true seeker to divine the fact that all spiritual techniques, including meditation, should serve only the limited objective of neutralizing the stresses within and the binding effects of the past. These techniques are thus only the 'means' to realize the ultimate objective (the 'end'), which should be effectiveness, clarity and harmony with all aspects within and without.

After all, the business of life is to get on with it. Excessive resort to such 'spiritual crutches', is often a sign of a disorder in one's very approach to life and in his ways of acting and thinking. It would therefore be necessary to be clear about one's priorities, utilizing these time-tested and powerful spiritual practices and techniques merely to integrate and harmonize all aspects of one's personality. In the clarity thus obtained, he should, sooner than later, evolve into briskness, flow and joyful work, which verily is worship and also a more powerful meditative technique — a true catharsis to the spirit within.

This also is the ultimate methodology to realize for oneself the final objective of all worthwhile living — being spiritual, while also simultaneously living with purpose and vision!

A Rendezvous with Cosmic Creativity

Vithal C Nadkarni

DR A VELUMANI, the founder of the Rs.500-crore Thyrocare Corp, had his 'aha' moment at a cancer hospital in Mumbai. As a doctoral student of thyroid chemistry at the Tata Memorial Hospital, everyday he used to see people camping on the road outside the hospital at Parel in Mumbai. These were relatives of patients who practically lived on the street because they did not have accommodation. This reminded him of the two nights he had spent on the CST railway platform when he first came to Mumbai from Tamil Nadu as a penniless youth.

Velumani also desperately wanted to mitigate the suffering of the patients and their relatives. Daily contact with suffering and anxiety had not deadened his sensitivity. Still, he was not a physician or surgeon. Nor was he a philanthropist with limitless funds at his disposal and he knew his mathematics alright — born in landless farmer's family, the brilliant math student had had to earn Rs.1.25 a day, plucking cotton at the tender age of eleven.

Then he had that moment of clarity in the cancer ward. This was what he now calls a rendezvous with cosmic creativity: He realized that his own USP was medical diagnostics, and this had to be the one service he would offer to patients without profiting at their expense.

Velumani's main justification for the low rate was that it rendered the 'sin' of having to make money out of patients less of a burden on his conscience (*Kam paap chahiye toh kam paisa le lo*). And his mantra to success was: "Do not focus on today's business, create tomorrow's big business; only see the runway, not the highway."

This was how he hit upon what he now calls the 'ethical' paradox of scale: "In the twelve years since I started Thyrocare, the cost of everything — rentals, fuel and reagents — had skyrocketed; yet my customers are not paying a single paisa more than they did twelve years ago," he says. "Initially, my competitors called me 'crazy' for the rates I charged. They waited for me to go bankrupt, but in vain."

What the competition had not figured out was that when one works with joyous abandon and tries to 'lose' something for the sake of one's patients the more one is likely to win, he adds, "Conversely, if one acts out of fear of losing something and is even willing to gouge one's patients only to protect the margins, the more likely are the chances of one's loss. This is as certain as the water from the Ganga flowing down to the Arabian Sea."

Trees, Rocks, Fish Fly to Nirvana Too

Vithal C Nadkarni

YASUHIRO HAMANO WAS three-years-old when his father took him on a fly-fishing expedition. In the secluded woods off Kyoto in the shadow of the Mist-Catcher Mountains, Hamano Sr enunciated his philosophy of 'Nature-vision concept' to his wide-eyed son: One could not exist without the other. You could not sustain a concept without vision, for example, which, in turn, needed Nature in order to be nurtured. Hamano Sr also introduced his son to the Zen-like mysteries of fly-fishing, and the intimate connection it bears to the environment ethic.

Years later, when he had made a mark as a multifaceted savant in architecture, fashion, design, photography, as well as philosophy and active adventure sports Hamano Jr rediscovered the principles he'd learnt as a budding fly-fisherman. "Every mountain stream has its resident rainbow trout with its own ecology," he told us in Mumbai in 2008. "There could be as many as 700 sorts of insects in various forms floating around for you to use as potential bait to snare this wily fish," he ruminated. "Which one to use and how, would be something that the wannabe angler has to negotiate between his hands, head and the all-encompassing field. Yet these very fishermen who are the most sensitive to these natural cycles have to ultimately transcend their fishing rods, and turn into guardians and sentries of the rivers and Nature herself," he emphasized. This flows out of the philosophy of the Tendai Sect which is akin to concepts of 'deep ecology', and is rooted in the idea that Buddhahood, or the capacity to attain enlightenment, is intrinsic in all things.

"Masters like Kukai and Saicho, for example, preached that plants, trees, rocks and everything else in this world has the quality of Buddha and will eventually reach nirvana. In other words, everything in this life is equal in Nature, and therefore fish and men are equal as well," he explained.

He also narrated the story of birth of Zen when the Buddha wordlessly held up a flower in an assembly. Nobody except Old Kashyapa reacted: "He alone smiled, as Buddha smiled back."

The Master's gesture can be interpreted as an invocation to use your hands for creative activity, rather than the mind. The philosophy is reflected in his projects such as Tokyu Hands and Friends of Rivers. It also explains why the Crow Tribe chief Mickey Old Coyote named him 'Travelling Wisdom' in Montana.

Enlightened Pursuit of Pleasure

Vithal C Nadkarni

FARMER SMITH BOUGHT a turkey poult for his yard. His young daughter became fond of the fuzzy little bird, which she plied with choice grains and greens. In less than three years, the cute chick had ballooned into a rotund bird that waddled around the farm like a feathered pumpkin.

After a thousand days of contentment, the very concept of fear had disappeared from the bird's brain just as it had from the mind of the Dodo, another bird that became fearless on an island Eden.

Then calamity struck. That year, it was the Smith family's turn to offer a bird for community Thanksgiving. Thus, the farmer Smith, who had otherwise been a paragon of virtue, became a mortal enemy of the poor bird.

The moral of the story is pretty stark — 'don't be fooled by the past, or even the present: for that's not the way to live in a world that one does not understand very well, says noted risk analyst and author of *Black Swan*, Nassim Nicholas Taleb in an essay.

Taleb was commenting on the current subprime crisis and on the limits of statistically-driven claims. By his take, when it comes to anticipating that comparatively rare event which can massively disrupt the predictable monotony of our lives, we humans seem to be as clueless about the future as 'little' Tom Turkey! Buddhists have extended that insight into the Doctrine of Anitya, which can also be partly summarized by the well-known adage — in life nothing is certain except death and taxes.

So how does one conduct oneself in a world that has death as the one great certainty which 'cures' the disease called life? Start by avoiding false attributions: which means we must not mistake what is essentially unstable and impermanent as something everlasting or perennial.

Does that demonize pursuit of pleasure, which is proverbially transient? Not really. Instead of blind pursuit we need an 'enlightened' approach. This explains why Indian tradition ranks *kama* or desire alongside *artha* (money) and *dharma* (duty) with *moksha* (liberation) among the four principal goals of human endeavour.

Enlightened pursuit of pleasure would therefore entail something like enjoying caviar with caveat, with the knowledge that the source of the commodity and its consumer are both mortally endangered entities! But knowledge alone cannot be an antidote to angst. Nor is it enough to get us off the carousel. For that you need detached but skilful action.

Empower Yourself with Divine Wisdom

Chaitanya Charan Das

IMAGINE YOURSELF ON a jaunt in a foreign land. Suddenly you see a person rushing towards you with both hands upraised shouting in an alien tongue. Instinctively you raise both hands to counter-attack. But that person rushes by you and you hear a heavy blow landing on someone. Surprised, you turn around and understanding dawns. A ruffian had been creeping up to attack you from behind and the person ahead had only been rushing to save you. He had been warning you in his foreign tongue, but being unable to comprehend his words you had completely misunderstood his intentions. Your regret? If only I had known his language...

Could this be the way we misunderstand God when problems suddenly rush into our lives? There is amazing intelligence that arranges for all our basic needs — air, heat, light, water and food. Equally awesome is the organization that enables all the life-sustaining bodily mechanisms like metabolism, respiration, blood circulation. Only after shedding intellectual sweat for centuries have scientists begun to understand partially the functioning of the universe.

Sadly, most people hardly spare even a thought to understand the purpose of the universe. And when things don't work out according to the plans they make in a few minutes or hours with the few grams of their puny brains, they conclude that God is perverse, negligent or non-existent. Like in the story above, they can't understand the language in which God is speaking to us.

Therefore, God gave us scriptures to serve as translators for us to understand His message and plan. The Vedic scriptures — and indeed all religious scriptures — assert unequivocally that God is our greatest well-wisher. Through them God alerts us of the imminent onslaught of misery, old age, disease and death. God's ultimate plan is to save us from all suffering and reinstate us in our eternal blissful life in His abode.

As a part of His plan, God often breaks things to transform them into something far more valuable. He breaks clouds to give rains, breaks soil to give grains, breaks grains to give bread and breaks bread to give nourishment. Similarly He sometimes has to break our plans for temporary material enjoyment to enrich us with everlasting devotional bliss. Therefore, the next time when providence seems to inimically charging at us, let us empower ourselves with divine wisdom to respond with faith and surrender.

Using Religion to Sell Science

Vithal C Nadkarni

LEON LEDERMAN HAD already won the Nobel Prize for physics when we met the former director of the Fermi National Accelerator Laboratory during the Intel science fair at San Jose in the US. After the meeting, we realized why some people called Professor Lederman a branding guru in disguise. In 1993, he published a book on fundamental physics called *God Particle* with science writer Dick Teresi. Of course, nobody had actually seen the *God Particle*. But then nobody had seen the bearded gent in the sky either although many on earth do claim to have direct access to Him.

Before Mr Lederman's christening coup, the *God Particle* had an infinitely more prosaic moniker — Higgs Boson — after Peter Higgs, the Scottish scientist who first proposed the existence of the particle which could tidy up some extremely messy aspects the Big Picture that particle physicists were trying to put together for decades. Mr Lederman said it made perfect sense to invoke the Almighty while re-naming the Higgs particle, because the mechanism that supposedly brought the particle into being made it possible to simplify the universe by resolving many seeming forces into One Unified whole.

He also likened it to tearing down the Tower of Babel, to put in its place one universal Lingua Franca of Nature. In passing, he also mentioned that his publisher had complained that nobody but nobody, had ever heard of the Higgs particle.

So was he deliberately using religion to sell science? Absolutely, he laughed, but without the equations! On a more serious note, he felt that the association had done nothing but good for physics. Hadn't Albert Einstein done the same? In the context of the many baffling paradoxes of quantum theory, the father of the Theory of Relativity had said, "The Lord is subtle, but malicious he is not."

So should we rule out divine intervention in the shutdown of the Large Hadron Collider, after its much-hyped launch? Some believers say it was His way of warning off physicists tinkering with fundamental questions about conversion of energy into matter and consciousness. "For heaven's sake it's just a helium leak," protest rationalists willing to put their faith in scientists' ability to recreate conditions of the Big Bang — the point at which our universe was thought to be created. If they fail they can always pray for inspiration, not to forget funding.

No Need to Finger the Moon

Mukul Sharma

ZEN OFTEN SAYS that all instruction is but a finger pointing to the moon and those whose gaze is fixed upon the pointer will never see beyond. "Even let them catch sight of the moon, and still they cannot see its beauty." It's another way of saying that the teaching is not the truth but merely an indicator towards it. In fact, Zen sums it up even better when it says, "A special transmission outside the scriptures; no dependence upon words and letters; direct pointing at the soul of man; seeing into one's nature and attainment of Buddhahood." The essential idea, thus, is to find whatever it is within oneself, not on the road. After all, if you meet the Buddha on the road you need to kill him, remember?

So can one not be pardoned for being confused when other Zen teachings also maintain that the journey is of greater significance than the arrival? That's the trouble with trying to be succinct to a fault. It's a trap that some masters of Zen, too, frequently fall into inadvertently. When you try to encapsulate an experience, idea or initiative into a few pithy words it can lead to confusion between the ears of the beholder.

Actually, we should know better because the same thing happens all the time with proverbs. 'Look before you leap is' is excellent advice for all concerned in every walk of life till someone else tells us that 'he who hesitates is lost' which suddenly also makes great sense for all concerned in every walk of life. And the examples are legion: What's good for the goose is good for the gander

One man's meat is another man's poison; The best things in life are free

There's no such thing as a free lunch; You're never too old to learn; You can't teach an old dog new tricks. Etc.

What's happening here is that we're getting carried away by the sound of our own mind as it tries to carve perceived, partial and half truths in stone. The truth may or may not be out there but its representation is made complete inside our heads in one way or another but always in a bipolar fashion. It might be better instead if we told ourselves that it's never too late to try to teach an old dog new tricks, or there are no such things as the best things in life or, even, he who leaps and hesitates is lost. Similarly, the finger — meaning the way — pointing to the moon — or destination — should perhaps be seen only as an indicator to itself because it too is the moon, and vice versa.

From Darkness to Light

K Vijayaraghavan

THE SECOND PART of the great universal prayer from Brahadaranyaka Upanishad (1,3,28) is for being led from darkness to light (*tamaso ma jyotir gamaya*). This is a logical follow-up of the first part, *asato ma sat gamaya.* 'Darkness', in the spirit of this prayer, connotes confusion or uncertainties — afflictions which could affect even highly evolved souls.

The natural guiding mechanism, which exists in us all, is enabled to flower forth through application, persistence and an abiding synthesis, which would invariably follow objective analysis of related issues. In this manner, this mechanism, the guiding force within, which verily is the guru within, enables the veil of such ignorance to be lifted for comprehending the path laid for oneself (*swadharma*) — the age-old concept of 'Know Thyself'. This also is the spirit of an ancient Sanskrit prayer, which pays obeisance to this guru, who, through imparting right knowledge, dispels the darkness within. This, in essence, is the process of being led from darkness to light.

Cardinal Newman's 'Lead Kindly Light', is one of the most inspiring poems written on this issue. Admitting that he is caught in an 'encircling gloom', the poem oozes with humility, through these lines.

"The night is dark and I am far from home:...
I do not ask to see
The distant scene, one step enough for me."

He also looks back,

"I was not ever thus, nor prayed that Thou
Shouldst lead me on, I loved to choose and see my path; but
Lead thou me on,
I loved the garish day, and, spite of fears,
Pride ruled my will: Remember not past years".

Self honesty and the desire for redemption also go with an abiding confidence that 'with the morn', those 'angel faces' would again smile, 'which I have loved long since, and lost awhile'.

It is in this spirit of being hopeful and loving, even when there does not appear a light at the end of the tunnel, which inspired Joyce Kilmer to write these great lines (Love's Lantern),

"Because the road was steep and long
And through a dark and lonely land,
God set upon my lips a song
And put a lantern in my hand."

The seeking spirit, wary of distractions, would also be guided in its prayers by the Biblical exhortation (John 12,35), 'Walk while you have the light, lest darkness come unto you'. This also is true enlightenment, through discovering the answers for the troubles that assail the mind. This, verily and essentially, is also the process of dispelling the darkness within (*tamas*) to emerge into eternal light (*jyoti*)!

The Agnostic's Path to Spiritualism

Mukul Sharma

SOCRATES SAID THAT an unexamined life is not worth living. Presumably he meant that given the amount of brains we have — stuff that's capable of developing tools, language and thought — it would seem a waste to use it the way lower animals with lesser gumption do. We could of course live out our existence like cows or cockroaches — with the addition of holding a job, seeing movies and some grocery shopping in between — or we could sit back sometimes and wonder what it's all about. The Greek philosopher was of the opinion that it might make our lives significantly more than outright worthless if we did so.

The problem is, Socrates didn't take believers and atheists who make up the bulk of humanity into account. For a believer, for instance, a life without examination can never be a life not worth living. That's because worth for that person is ordained in birth and built upon a faith that conflicts with any subsequent inquiry. In fact, the only thing which needs to be reflected upon at all is whether one has led the life the scriptures have enjoined and, if not, what needs to be done to get back on track. With a god, any inquiry is only the study of divine commands. Which brings us to atheists.

If Kierkegaard defined faith as the leap taken despite everything, despite the very absurdity of what one is asked to believe, then atheists take the same leap backwards into the very mouth of absurdity and disbelief. And when you've done something like that and are reconciled to it, what's left to examine? If life's just a chancy one-off biochemical epiphenomenon in an overall godless structure then, forget worth, what value can any meaning — if such a thing itself means anything, that is — ever have? Without God, any inquiry is ultimately lifeless. Which brings us to agnostics.

Is this where Socrates was coming from? It must be. But not the type of fence-sitter who after taking the high amoral ground promptly abdicates all further mental inquiry and pretty much behaves and lives the life that people at the polar ends of the continuum do. No, what the man had in mind is what some people call spiritual agnosticism where the spirit of inquiry and examination is never abandoned but is used to gain perspective over values and to engage in ideas rather than simply accepting them. In its highest form this approaches mysticism but, even otherwise, it's fundamentally an enduring search for quality.

Purpose Behind & Nature of Prayer

K Vijayaraghavan

THAT NEEDED 'EXTRA touch', which could often make the difference between mere earnest attempt and true fulfilment to one's quest is imparted through adoption of the most suited prayer for each particular situation, need or individual. This serves as the impetus and inspiration in trying and depressing situations, which anyone who treads the path of excellence would necessarily have to encounter.

The type of prayer, entreaty or supplication could vary from the devout who may choose one that is addressed to a deity or object of worship to the agnostic who may simply summon a will or wish within. Whatever be the methodology or choice adopted, this earnest approach would necessarily involve mustering the abiding will and wish power within (*iccha shakti*), or resolution (*sankalpa*) which would naturally obtain for the seeker the power to get the needed knowledge (*gnana shakti*). This would invariably culminate in the happy conclusion of final consummation of gain
power for truly realizing the actual desired objective (*kriya*
This indeed is the awesome power of prayer, epitomized
immortal lines (The Passing of Arthur) of Tennyson

'More things are wrought by prayer
Than the world dreams of'.

The purpose behind adopting this entreaty, supplicat
shakti or prayer — by whatever term one may choose to

is thus the integration of the various forces in the conscious, subconscious and the unconscious. Right analysis and true synthesis, which would invariably follow, would guide the aspirant to act well, rightly and wisely to take the effective and unhindered route to his objective, obtaining support of forces and nature, all over. This is also the translation of the ancient concept of Aeschylus, 'When a man is willing and eager, the gods join in.' This assured support is also conceived of by the Bible (Luke -11, 9; also Mathew - 7,8) 'Ask and it shall be given to you; seek and you shall find; knock and it shall be opened unto you.'

This manner of earnest seeking, involving the right nature and type of supplication, would be endearingly supportive when nobility of the objective envisioned also goes with that abiding sincerity within. Welfare and benefit to oneself, when extended to goodness and peace to the world around, is the key to this noble approach. Benefits are never conceived of, in this spirit, at the expense of anything or anyone else. This, verily, is true prayer and sublime praying!

The Non-existent Great Divide

Mukul Sharma

ACCORDING TO OWEN Gingerich, former research professor of Astronomy and History of Science at Harvard University, there's an easy way out of the unholy science versus religion divide — but it takes brains, not ideological brawns, to see it. As one reviewer of his book, *God's Universe*, put it: there are two ways to think about science. You can be a theist, believing that behind the veil of randomness lurks an active, loving, manipulative God, or you can be a materialist, for whom everything is matter and energy interacting within space and time. Whichever metaphysical club you belong to, the science comes out the same. And, in the process, religion still remains viable.

Meaning, one can be like the British philosopher Anthony Flew — once dubbed the world's most notorious atheist — who, at the age of 81 suddenly decided that the structure of the DNA molecule was simply too complex to have arisen purely out of a range of probabilities, and accepted God. Or one can be like the hundreds of hopeful young genetic scientists who beaver away on unravelling the intricacies of gene mapping believing that random chance just happened to be extremely lucky in producing the unique result(s) we see, without the need for any divine intervention or interest.

The point is, either way coexistence is not a problem. It only becomes one when one side will not leave the other alone. When for instance someone like the evolutionary biologist Richard

Dawkins of *The God Delusion* fame continues to publicly flay those who have faith as being somehow intellectually less robust and emotionally more fragile. Or when some institution like the Papal office condemns genetic modification as one of the seven deadly new sins or 'capital vices' as it calls them.

Actually coexistence doesn't have to be a problem at all. That is, if we believe in a designed universe but not in the concept of Intelligent Design, the fake-scientific front of creationism. Instead, let's look at design as an emergent property of the universe. In the beginning there was only an un-patterned quantum fluctuation in the void which escalated outwards and along the way produced many configurations and arrangements between parts of itself. Some of these resulted in finely structured galaxies and planets, some in living organisms, and some in consciousnesses which are capable of conjuring up such coherent scenarios.

Detached Practice Leads to Perfection

Vithal C Nadkarni

IN THE EARLY years of their discovery, X-rays were a rage in fashionable society. People got X-rayed the way they had photographs. All this changed once the deadly effects of the radiation came to light. Grimacing skull and cross-bones thus became associated with the radiation that practically launched the 20th century. In the following decades radiologists turned to other emissions and atomic effects to get over these limitations.

The boffins are now able to capture bodily tissues and processes in action. Tomography and magnetic scanning have grown so sophisticated that these days some scientists are even trying to capture the wiliest wisps of thoughts, base or transcendent, on film. This may explain why someone like Dr Andrew Newberg has the polysyllabic designation of professor of radiology, psychology and religious studies at the University of Pennsylvania.

Dr Newberg is also the cofounder of Penn's Centre for Spirituality and the Mind. Studies of worshipful and contemplative states have led him to author four books including *How God Changes Your Brain.* Regular meditation what Patanjali's *Yoga Sutra* calls prolonged uninterrupted — *dirgha nairantaira* — practice does cause permanent changes in the brain just as the yogis promise; meditators who stuck out for 15 or more years appear to have thicker frontal lobes of the brain. This in turn seems to boost concentration and memory.

Even cursory training seemed to cause measurable physiological change: brain scans of people who complained of poor recall before and after undergoing meditation training revealed bulking up of the brain lobes, which had discernible mnemonic improvement. The secret of the process is laid bare in a well-known *doha* attributed to the mystic poet Kabir: If one persists long enough, even the hardest rock of inertia and ill-being can be cut with the softest silk of practice:

Karat karat abhyasa-ke jada-mati hota sujaan
Jaise aawat-jaawat rasari-ke shil par hot nisaan.

The key concept offered by Kabir as also by *the Bhagavad Gita* is *abhyasa*. This entails having the right attitude of persistent effort to attain a state of stable tranquillity. But for right practice or *abhyasa* to succeed, one also needs *vairagya* or detachment. This involves letting go of needless fears and fixes. Detached practice thus opens the path to perfection.

Experience His Liberating Presence

Vithal C Nadkarni

AN E-MAIL FROM a friend talks about what is arguably the lighter side of recession. It starts with a joke about Messrs Ali Baba and Forty Thieves being rebranded as 'Ali Baba and Thirty Thieves' because of ten lay-offs! And it goes on to describe the only deposits being made on a Ferrari these days as those made by birds flying over the car!

Another e-mailer directed your columnist to an essay in *The New York Times* that talks about how a seemingly substantial $500,000 'goes faster than one might think': Allen Salkin starts by itemizing expenses such as mortgage and coop apartment maintenance fee (each $96,000 a year); nanny and private school ($45,000 and $32,000 per year respectively). "We are already at $269,000, and we haven't even gotten to taxes yet," he adds, explaining that 'the $500,000 is the amount President Barack Obama wants to set as pay (excluding bonuses and incentives) for bank executives whose firms accept government bail-out money'. Clearly those who accept handouts cannot be choosers in secular, read hard-headed economic, terms.

Mercifully, the spiritual traditions around the world seem to believe otherwise. In his Sermon on The Mount, Jesus famously proclaims, "Blessed are you who are poor, for yours is the kingdom of God." Of course, those entitled to draw a half-million dollar pay packet aren't exactly 'poor' unless they are comparing themselves to those who can afford to spend the entire amount on a bauble or too. Still, it's reassuring to hear from the Lord that 'blessed are those who are hungry for you will be befitted'; not perhaps with caviar and champagne, but certainly with divine bread and sardines, and don't forget the water, which He in his infinite mercy turned to wine! No wonder Mahatma Gandhi once said reading the 'Sermon on The Mount' gave him comfort and boundless joy!

A similar sentiment can be found in the celebrated prayer of Queen Kunti from The Bhagvatam: After recounting her escape from arsonists, cannibals, royal rapists, murderous generals and exile in the forest only due to Sri Krishna's deliverance, Kunti prays to the Lord that all those calamities return so that she may experience His liberating presence again and again, while entreating Him as the Lord of the Poor (*Akinchana-gocharam*) and Wealth of the Poor (*Akinchanavittaya*), beyond zillions.

The Trouble with True Detachment

Mukul Sharma

ONE DOESN'T HAVE to be contrarian or ornery to observe that selfless action of the kind advocated by some of our wisest minds can be a bit of a pain to actually operationalize. The Hindu saint Mata Amritanandamayi says, "The beauty and charm of selfless love and service should not die away from the face of the Earth.... Through selfless action we can eradicate the ego that conceals the Self. Detached, selfless action leads to liberation. Such action is not just work; it is karma yoga." Yet, focusing on the adherence to duty or dharma while remaining detached from the reward often seems almost impossible to achieve. Consider for instance the following true story.

A man used to go jogging regularly in a park every morning. As usually happens in such cases, he came across almost the same faces everyday — people out early for workouts, pleasure or just enjoying a part of the day before work. One morning, however, he saw something completely different. Pedalling furiously down the cycle track from the other side was a man on a bicycle with a large and rather ferocious looking eagle perched on the handlebar in front of him. The bird had its head and beak jutting into the wind while its wings were spread out on either side, spanning the entire front of the cycle like an oversized emblem. The two swept past the jogger and disappeared down the track.

He saw them everyday after that and each time it was the same scenario: man trying to cycle as fast as he could with bird perched in front of him, its wings skimming the onrushing air. The mystery was finally solved when he found the exhausted cyclist taking a break on the grass. The eagle was sitting on his shoulder. Between gasps he replied that his pet had broken its wings in an accident many years ago and couldn't fly any more. Feeling that a hunting animal must be missing such a deep an instinctual activity, he tried to do the next best thing to simulate flight. On the handlebar with the cycle going full tilt the eagle probably got the impression it was soaring by itself.

The question is, how selfless was this otherwise utterly compassionate activity? That it was done totally out of love and devotion cannot be doubted for a moment. At the same time, to what extent was there any real detachment from the perceived reward? Truth to tell, hardly any. It was, simultaneously, an absolute adherence to duty with virtually no indifference involved.

Evolution Can Coexist with God

Mukul Sharma

THE YEAR 2009 was the 200th anniversary of Charles Darwin's birth and the 150th anniversary of the publication of his *Origin of Species* which gave birth to the theory of evolution. Simply put, it states that change in the genetic composition of a population during successive generations as a result of natural selection acting on the variation among individuals results in the development of new species. In one brilliant flash of insight and sustained reasoning, Darwin demolished forever the idea that some divine creator made all the different species of animals and plants that have ever existed. A century and a half later, developments in the field of genetics and DNA have only confirmed the theory's basic tenets.

Of course, there's been resistance. In his own day Darwin was savagely attacked by people who felt threatened by what they perceived as not only a frontal attack on their fundamental religious beliefs but because evolution dethroned humans from their pedestal. No longer could man be considered the pinnacle of all creatures built for a godly purpose; he was just a blind by-product in the normal course of life's development. It was as shattering a blow as that delivered by Nicolaus Copernicus when his scientifically based heliocentric cosmology displaced the Earth from the centre of the universe to a bit player on the sidelines of one among billions of galaxies.

Even today, empirically illiterate creationists along with their so-called 'scientific' Intelligent Design contemporaries keep assailing evolution for being 'just a theory' which should be taught in schools along with all other theories of the creation of different species. In the process they conveniently forget that the Theory of Relativity and the Theory of Gravitation are also 'only theories'. They never attack those because who wants to jump off a building to prove one of them wrong.

So does this mean God cannot coexist with evolution? Not at all. As far as believers are concerned they should understand that Darwin never attempted to explain how life itself first came to be nor how it originally arose from inanimate carbon compounds to become living matter. Darwin was also agnostic towards the existence of consciousness and mind. And till such time as science can explain such things they must remain the subject of philosophy and religion. Life can reach well beyond science, without coming into conflict with it.

Liberate Yourself with Detachment

Vithal C Nadkarni

FOLKLORE TALKS OF the faithful cow and the kind tiger. This was from the days when animals spoke like humans. Perhaps they still do. But shamans say we've lost the key: Nobel-Prize-winner ethologist Konrad Lorenz calls it King Solomon's ring, which lets us into the secrets of another species' speech.

In the story, a cow used to feed in a big forest all by herself. One day on her way back, she met a hungry tiger. The tiger wanted to eat her up at once, but the cow told the beast she had a nursing calf at home and that was hungry too. She pleaded with the tiger to let her off while promising to return after she had fed the calf. She repeated the promise three times and the tiger let her go.

The cow returned to the tiger as promised after feeding the calf, which came running and bawling after the mother with tears streaming down its face. 'Eat me instead,' it pleaded.

The tiger couldn't believe that mother and son had come back to face certain death. Moved by pity, the big cat let the pair go. The conventional moral of the story is: "Always keep your word, for it pays!" But that does not fully explain why the story moves so many listeners to tears. Of course they are not naïve: in the real world, tigers kill cows straying into their territory, just as wardens have to fork out compensation to save the tigers from the wrath of the villagers.

In poetic contrast, in the imagined world, even dumb animals strive to do the right thing in the face of colossal odds crafted by Nature and Nurture. Now, that may be a lesson — it's better to die than to subvert moral order — which is worthy of respect from all-too-fallible men.

The question then is whose heroics are greater. Is it the cow overriding maternal instincts and willingly returning to her predator? Or is it the tiger who still gives up his 'steaks-on-hooves' dinner while knowing fully that he cannot survive on grass and goodwill alone? Interestingly, a Sanskrit version of the story found in the Shanti-Parva of *Mahabharata* tacitly makes a bow to laws according to Darwin, when it sends all three dramatis personae, bovine and feline, to heaven for their exemplary adherence to principle!

One interpretation is that he who practices transcendental unselfishness has no place on Earth. He belongs to the world of bloodless angels. It takes Lordly wisdom to reverse that message in the *Bhagavad Gita*: with detachment you can liberate yourself, here and now.

Persevere in Your Spiritual Quest

Vithal C Nadkarni

THE MOTTO OF 'service before self' epitomized the life of Swami Chidananda Saraswati, who passed away in 2008 at the age of 92. Swamiji was often called the St Francis of India after the great Franciscan monk, St Francis of Assissi, of whom the austere monk was himself deeply attracted to. He served as president of the Divine Life Society which has centres across the globe for more than forty years from 1963 and he nurtured Vedantic tradition in these turbulent times, much like his own master Sivananda.

As one of India's representatives at the centenary of the World Parliament of Religions in 1993, Swamiji said it was 'a rare blessedness and a great good to enter into the spiritual life. And to take it seriously and engage in active spiritual *sadhana* was a second blessedness and a still greater good,' he added.

"But to persevere and to be ever progressive and ceaseless in one's spiritual life was the greatest good; the crowning blessedness," he said. His own life was a living testimony to the great ancient ideals he reiterated for the modern age.

In a discourse on living the Divine Life, he said it meant living in the awareness that you are essentially divine, that your real being is timeless and eternal. That Supreme Cosmic Reality remains one and non-dual regardless of place of worship and is the same One glorified in all the world's scriptures and religions, he said.

Nor did you need to renounce the world to lead a Divine Life, he explained further, because even while living your normal domestic, professional and social life, you can attain your goal. "But first you must purify your heart and rid it of narrow selfishness by dedicated service to others. Be ever eager to serve all — the sick, the poor, the suffering and the sorrowful," he exhorted.

"Feel blessed by every opportunity to serve your fellow beings and all of God's creatures on the planet. From this motiveless selfless service comes a pure heart," he affirmed, "which in turn brings devotion to God."

"Secondly, worship the Supreme daily, for That is the centre of your existence. That is not far away from you," he said, "but is the ever-present Divine Spirit pervading this entire universe. That is closer to you than your very breath. Never forget this. This process of daily worship and prayer has the power to gradually steady the restless mind, to overcome its fickle nature and bring concentration."

Rewards of True Spirituality

K Vijayaraghavan

WHENEVER THE SEEKER takes up any exercise in personality development, including any specific spiritual or meditative technique, he should be watchful of possible mindsets, whereby he could easily bring himself to be 'convinced' that he has achieved a breakthrough. In actual fact, he may be traversing the same ground, which he had done thus far. The perceived benefits may thus be illusory!

When the seeker comprehends that the acid test to any spiritual progress is obtaining greater clarity and effectiveness, he would not be blown over or blinded by ill-founded opinions or perceptions from within or without. Retaining for himself that needed faith and trust in the time-tested techniques, he would also be guided by a healthy scepticism and open-mindedness that would enable him to divine if he has to change track and if, in actual fact, each tomorrow finds him 'farther than today' (to use the phrase of HW Longfellow).

Choosing the right technique through observation, analysis and synthesis, the practitioner would divine the means to resolve the various retarding forces within. Patanjali in his *Yoga Sutra* (1,30), lists ten 'enemies to yoga'. Emphasizing (1,32) that it is necessary to practice on one truth, he also prescribes (1,33) the right approach to each particular aspect of life. This is akin to the modern cognitive behaviour therapy.

Patanjali's concept of observance of basic rules of living (*yama, niyama*), besides elucidation of performance of postures with right approach, whereby stresses and conflicts are resolved — these give further guidelines of adoption of a multi-pronged approach to spiritual and thus effective and worthwhile living. Each aspirant should, depending on his own nature, comprehend the right approach, as suited to him.

In short, specific spiritual exercises or meditation should act in harmony with other aspects too, which also are vitally necessary — right approach, lifestyle, habits including those on sleep and food and being vigilant of distraction or acts of slip up. The seeker thus integrates all aspects of his life through a virtuous cycle. Liberated of all the binding forces within and without, he discovers for himself the potential and power within — discovery of one's true self and thus one's work upon this earth. This is attainment of 'flow', where work is its own reward — a catharsis or a meditative exercise by itself. This ultimately is the well-earned reward of a truly spiritual life.

Have Faith, But First Do Your Work

K Vijayaraghavan

THE CONCLUDING STANZA (18, 78) of *the Bhagavad Gita* is on the invincible combination of the 'lord of yoga', Krishna and the 'bow wielding' Arjuna, which would always bring about prosperity, success and established morality. The adjective, 'bow wielding', presupposes that human aspirations have necessarily also to go with that willingness and capacity to persevere, working not merely hard but also intelligently and with a sense of direction. It is in this situation that external situations or developments, nature's support and divine grace also join in as allies in the aspirant's pursuit. Rightly was it said that God helps those who help themselves.

The capacity for infinite patience and intent, thus, also has to go with capacity for taking infinite pains — the concept of 98 per cent perspiration and two per cent inspiration. HW Longfellow's concept, in his A Psalm of Life, 'learn to labour and to wait', is preceded by his earlier lines,

"Let us, then, be up and doing,
With a heart for any fate"

and also 'his own supreme' lines in The Ladders of St Augustine,

"The heights by great men reached and kept
Were not attained by sudden flight,
But they, while their companions slept,
Were toiling upward in the night."

It is in the above regard that these lines of WE Henley (Invictus) assume immense significance — 'I am the master of my fate: I am the captain of my soul'.

No doubt, limitations of situations around, including compulsions, commitments and also lack of means could act as stumbling blocks. Some believe that destiny, karma and planetary positions, beside certain occult influences, are actually insurmountable obstacles. But then, free will and intensity of the yearning within could overcome these through right application through obtaining that glowing wisdom (*jnanagni*), which, as *the Bhagavad Gita* notes, (4,37), reduces to ashes, the binding effects of all karma.

Fatalism or inaction, under the cover of destiny are thus, often, alibis for failure and escape routes for the weak in spirit. Dynamic optimism, on the other hand, and that willingness 'to labour and to wait', besides that abiding capacity to smile even 'when everything goes dead wrong' (to use the inspiring expression of Ella Wheeler Wilcox) — these are the all conquering weapons in the armoury of the great to transcend barriers. It is in this manner that, to a seeking mind, in spite of frustrations on the way, answers will come — slowly and in stages perhaps, but certainly, surely and clearly.

Real Power Works From Deep Within

K Vijayaraghavan

PRACTICAL APPLICATION OF the law of optimum effort is divining that art of striking a golden mean between trying too much and trying too little and also that of striking the right balance between being too easygoing and being too serious or concerned about everything. This approach does not mean dilution of effort in any way. Indeed, this is also the working of an abiding, effective and powerful action that works from deep within, which does not, ever, have to manifest itself through boisterous or feverish activities. Rooted in an abiding wish power (*iccha shakti*), the seeker inevitably obtains for himself the needed knowledge (*gnana shakti*), and finally the wherewithal and means (*kriya sakti*) to finally obtain actually the desired objective itself.

The manner in which such inscrutable laws of human excellence and accomplishment work practically, is only too obvious in everyday life. It could be the case of a self-abnegating and caring housewife, who effectively attends to various pressing chores and demands, without ever appearing the worse in bringing out tangible results, which are only too apparent or the case of a musician, who strikes the right chords of melody as if effortlessly. Deep within is always the background of right training, assimilation, approach and attitude.

Excellence in sports too is often manifest in what, to an untrained eye, may appear as languid movements or a carefree approach.

Behind such external appearances would often actually lie the essence of accumulated efforts, spread over years of perseverance and persistence.

John Anderson in a highly illuminating article, 'What makes Olympic Champions' (Reader's Digest; September, 1994) analyses and elaborates on this fascinating subject. He concludes: "As you watch an Olympic champion perform on TV, look beyond his running or his leaps and loops. In these manoeuvres and superb performances, you can see qualities less easily measurable — qualities we can learn from, qualities for our children to imitate."

Elaborations as above and an understanding of the related issues would enable one to divine the secret and inner stories behind all accomplishments. These involve and are centred on that awesome power, which, bestowing on its possessor an outward calmness and elegance, in actuality, also works powerfully from deep within. Regardless of the manner in which it manifests to different eyes, this goes to produce golden moments of human excellence.

Spiritual Solution to Economic Problems

Acharya Mahaprajna

THE SOURCES OF problems lie both in the material world as well as in the intrinsic world of consciousness. Bhagwan Mahavira was a mantradata — a preceptor of short-cuts to precise solutions to intricate problems. One of his mantras to solve problems was based on the principle of bringing harmony between two extremes. So he said, "One who is cognisant of the intrinsic is cognisant of the extrinsic; one who is cognisant of the extrinsic is cognisant of the intrinsic." Hence, the intrinsic correlates with the spirituality, while the extrinsic with the external or physical conditions.

Now, there are some people who assert that the spirituality holds the key to all problems, while others insist on bringing about change in the external conditions for solving all problems. In fact, a holistic approach would be that it is imperative to change the external conditions as well as the internal ones. The two great challenges of the present day world are unlimited personal wealth and unlimited consumption.

On account of limitless individual possession, one section of the society is becoming more and more affluent, whereas another section of the society is becoming deprived and reeling under the agony of extreme poverty and hunger. For solving these two prime challenges, two mantras enunciated by Bhagwan Mahavira can prove extremely effective.

Putting a limit on one's possessions: The first and foremost vow of the code of conduct for a householder is to put a limit on one's own accumulation of wealth. The vow of non-possession cannot be prescribed for a householder. For, an individual totally devoid of possessions cannot make material and economic development, nor can he solve the problem of hunger.

Putting a limit to one's consumption: The second vow is to put a voluntary limit to one's individual consumption. One of the main causes of the environmental pollution is overconsumption or unnecessary consumption. Attachments to sensuality, the exhibition of pomp and show, expansion of the mentality to seek more and more comforts and the like — all these have led to imbalances in nature. Scientists and heads of nations are striving hard to solve the problems of the external world. But little change is visible.

Now, if efforts for bringing about internal change are coupled with those for external one and training is started to a change in the human consciousness, then better results can be gained in attaining success in solving the problems.

The Divine Self Lives Within You

Vithal C Nadkarni

THE LITTLE BOOK came by post. The title on the blue jacket simply said Bodhvachne (aphorisms of wisdom) of Sri Brahmachaitanya Gondvalekar Maharaj. There was also a picture of the saint in *ardha-padmasana* on a deer skin holding up a rosary. The compiler described himself as 'a learned fool' (*padhatmurkha*) *shishya* of the master.

That artless epithet struck a chord in your correspondent. But the message conveyed by each of the gemlike 1,000 aphorisms seemed even more powerful. Here was a guru from the Dattatreya Sampradaya, who had left his mortal coil one year before the start of the First World War. Yet his message was clear and fresh, as relevant today as it was when the Master delivered it to a world without internet or fax.

"Sri Gondvalekar Maharaj was repeating what the Great Acharya (Adi Shankarachaya) taught in Sanskrit and what Sri Jnandevmouli ('Mother' saint of the Warkaris) reiterated in Marathi for the masses," wrote one devotee. "Namasadhana or using the chant or the Name was for him the means of realizing one's divine nature *Tat tvam asi.* This could happen suddenly (*shaktipat*) or slowly at the pace of an ant."

That evoked a story: A seeker once went to a master and asked to be initiated into enlightenment. The master replied, "*Tat tvam asi,* you are That. The divine self lives within you. Meditate on that Self, merge in that Self, realize that Self."

"Is that all?" said the disappointed seeker. "But I already know that. Please reveal to me the inner secrets, the real stuff!" The master replied, "That is all I know. This is the entire caboodle. I have no other secret. But since you don't seem to be satisfied, try the master who lives down the road."

The pupil hurried to the other guru and posed the same question. "I do not part with my teachings so easily," replied the teacher. "You've got to earn them with sincere *sadhana* for 12 years."

The seeker agreed at once and was assigned to clean the cowsheds as part of *sadhana* day after day. Thus the years went by, with the seeker dreaming of enlightenment as he shovelled cowdung everyday. Finally, the great day arrived and the seeker ran up to the Master who said, "Oh Son! How well you've served me. So here it is: *Tat tvam asi*; Know it, meditate on it; merge into it."

"Is that all?" cried the enraged seeker. "But that's exactly what the first guru said."

"Well," the guru replied. "The truth hasn't changed in 12 years!"

Discovering One's 'Truest Interest'

K Vijayaraghavan

THE PRAYER EVOLVED by Benjamin Franklin beseeches the 'powerful Goodness, bountiful Father and merciful Guide' to increase in him that wisdom 'which discovers my truest interest'.

The age-old search of every seeking spirit has been in divining that vocation and pursuit specifically suited to it, which would not merely confer fulfilment but also that 'flow' and supreme effectiveness. This, verily, is the ultimate realization of all human quest through the call within — one's *swadharma*, or his work upon this Earth.

This quest, in essence is the entreaty, summed up beautifully in the great Indian prayer, *tamaso ma jyotir gamaya* and the inspiring poem of Cardinal Newman, commencing with the lines, Lead Kindly Light. This also is that approach, prompted by the ancient dictum, Know Thyself, inspired by the continual inquiry within, Quo Vadis. The entire process is centred on obtaining that supreme felicity of self-knowledge, self-realisation or *atmagnanam* — call what you will.

Philosophers — modern and ancient — over the entire world, have dealt with this sublime, though abstract subject and philosophy, in various ways. One example in this regard, is Somerset Maugham's portrayal of his characters, Charles Strickland and Abraham in his *Moon and Sixpence* and Larry Darrel in his *Razor's Edge*. Spurred on by the call within, they forsake sinecure living to pursue and fulfil their dreams, braving and overcoming difficulties from all over.

The sine-quo-non for all spiritual pursuits is thus knowing oneself and thus being clear in priorities and pursuits.

This 'knowing' comes not through just mere learning (*apara vidya*) but through that knowledge of the self, leading also to comprehending one's 'truest interest' (*para vidya*). The evolved seeker would not only 'act while there yet is time' but act also well, wisely and rightly.

This also would ensure that after obtaining the object of one's dreams, he would also always cherish and be fulfilled by what he has thus obtained. He would never, ever, have to feel, 'It is, but hadn't ought to be', as felt by the characters of Bret Harte's parody of John Whittier's Maud Muller.

The true essence of all spiritual pursuit is thus centred on that supreme blessing which any human can aspire for — realizing oneself and thus one's own 'truest interest'!

Unifying Saga of the Stone

Vithal C Nadkarni

THE SMALL CYLINDRICAL stone has been polished smooth in the river Narmada for aeons. It's like a chocolate *lingam* marked with delicate black lines. As I pay for it at the Crafts Museum in Delhi, the lady at the counter asks if it's for worship.

The stone's symmetry represents for me the essence of change. I imagine that when it first hurtled down into Narmada from the Vindhya Mountains, dinosaurs roamed the banks of the river. Then a fire must have come down from the skies, spreading darkness at noon and death among the saurians great and small. Mammals took their place. Neolithic human settlements appeared only 35,000 years ago. Through all this, the baby rock slept on unperturbed in the river. Still, it was being ground down, atom by atom, by the awesome forces of what is arguably the oldest river on earth.

When I unpack the stone at home in Mumbai, Mom's reactions remind me of what had been said at the Museum. She whisks the nut-brown banded pebble out of my hands. She touches it with a drop of sparkling Gangajal from a small silver jug kept in the family shrine and flecks it with vermilion and turmeric powder, before placing it reverentially in a *yoni*-shaped brassware stand that's stood empty for as long as I can remember.

"You've brought home a Narmadeshwar," she says. "We now have a complete Shiva-Shakti pair."

"But I bought it from a gift shop in Delhi," I argue. "All that is allowed, as long as you picked it up yourself during a journey to the North," Mom replies. For this is just what the tradition enjoins for Narmada stones revered all over India as sacred symbols of Siva.

I discover later that it was the organizing genius of Adi Shankaracharya who formalized the practice and gave it great spiritual weight in daily worship. "By doing so, the far-sighted Acharya turned these seemingly humble stones into icons of great geographical and religious unity for India at an extremely turbulent moment of her history," says Parivrajak Swami Gyanananda Saraswati, founder president of the Shankaracharya Vedic Research Centre in Varanasi. He was in Mumbai last month to celebrate 'Shankaravataranam', the 2514th birth anniversary of the Great Unifier. The Acharya was a champion of Advaita or Oneness so inclusive that it transcends all boundaries and labels. Yet it also exists as the eternal truth — Brahma Satyam — that even a little polished rock can symbolize and reflect back.

Irresolvable Paradox of Life & Death

Vithal C Nadkarni

THE MIND RECOILS at the images of Mumbai's iconic buildings burning in terrorist fire. Memories of similar attacks on other iconic structures in other cities are evoked. This brings to mind a still older memory of a magical afternoon one has spent with loved ones on the terrace of one of the Twin Towers, something that exists only as a neural trace in the brain today.

One also remembers how exactly one year after the catastrophe, in a moving ceremony on Ground Zero in downtown New York, three psychologists had presented a new theory. Called Terror Management Theory (TMT), the theoretical framework analysed our response to extremist attacks. The first reaction was said to be one of shock and disbelief or an inability to absorb the reality of attack. This was reflected in Sonia Gandhi's very first reaction to the media about the latest terrorist attack on Mumbai.

The second reaction, according to Sheldon Solomon, Jeff Greenberg and Tom Pyszczynski, the creators of TMT, involves searching for any distraction just so that one could take off one's mind from the cognitive enormity posed by the terrorist challenge. The third tendency, they went on to add, entailed withdrawal from society, and also taking some sort of protective action should more attacks recur.

The authors of TMT expressed their gratitude to the work of the late Ernst Becker, a Pulitzer-winning anthropologist who had written eloquently about humankind's denial of death and its far reaching consequences. In his posthumously published classic, *Escape from Evil*, for example, Becker showed how potent reminders of one's own mortality often provoked a belief in some sort of mystical transcendence involving otherworldly ideas of heaven, reincarnation or spiritualism.

Becker's own theory drew extensively on the insights of Otto Rank and philosopher Soren Kierkegaard. It tackled head on the so-called 'irresolvable paradox' created by the desire to preserve life and the realization of its ultimate futility (because of the certainty of death and taxes).

TMT begins with the premise that unlike animals, humans are aware of the certainty of their own death. Culture, which provides us a sense of meaning, organization and continuity, helps in coping with this psychological terror. The downside is that it also primes us for 'my system is better than yours' sort of wars that we are now witnessing.

We & Science

What do you think about science? Do you think that it has just unravelled the mysteries of the universe to us, paved the way for new inventions and discoveries, propounded theories and given us insight into natural phenomena? Or does science mean to you more than all this?

The articles in the section 'We & Science' describe how science has influenced our lives and thinking. The human brain has discovered and invented many things. Thus it is the creative instinct of the human mind which is responsible for all changes.

William Paley, the 18th-century philosopher, popularized the watchmaker analogy, which says that human artefacts are products of intelligent design and the universe resembles such artefacts. But the universe is vastly more complex and it must have been designed by a more powerful designer. According to the watchmaker analogy, just like the design of a watch implies a designer, so does the design of the universe.

One essay in this section explains why The Centre for the Study of Science and Religion was created. According to it, sciences respond to the felt need to understand the world, and religions respond to a felt need for the world to have meaning.

We may have made great progress in science and technology but even today 85 per cent of people stick to their belief in God. 'We & Science' explains the theory that there is a 'spiritual' aspect of DNA that makes us hold to these beliefs. We may or may not be able to justify them but most people continue to maintain their faith in God or a higher power, notwithstanding the strides we have made in the field of science.

Human Creativity, the Mother of All Changes

Vithal C Nadkarni

SPARE A THOUGHT FOR future prospects in the New Year. What would be the metatrend of the new season? Defined as a transformational or transcendent phenomenon, a metatrend goes beyond large changes caused by a mega trend. Moving from a bullock cart to a bullet train, for example, entails a large change. But it's not transformational in the sense of a cave painting being morphed into a moving image with optical technology.

At a physical level, the hand that produced the Altamira cave paintings is no different from the one that runs a camcorder. The difference yawns at the conceptual level. But it's not unbridgeable. A Neolithic hunter has the brain potential to master Relativity Theory. That is why some futurists look upon human ingenuity or adaptability itself as the transcendent metatrend. Human creativity is the mother of all transformative trends such as cultural modernization, economic globalization and universal connectivity.

More intriguing, humans seem to be getting smarter with every passing year: in the 1980s, an American academic named James Flynn found that average IQ scores in every industrialized country on the planet had been increasing steadily for decades. Recent studies indicate that the rate of increase may be accelerating. "Though the Flynn effect is now widely accepted, its existence raises new questions," says Steven Johnson, author of *Emergence: The*

Connected Lives Of Ants, Brains And Cities. "The phenomenon would seem to make no sense in light of the evidence that g (general intelligence) is largely an inherited trait. We're certainly not evolving that quickly."

He connects the IQ level hikes to the explosion of new technologies and interfaces in the last fifty years. Human brains seem to be adapting to the challenges posed by the new media. The hypothesis will be tested when the generation raised on hypertext and massively complex game worlds starts taking adult IQ tests.

"This is a generation who, in many cases, learned to puzzle through the visual patterns of graphic interfaces before they learned to read," Mr Johnson writes. "Their fundamental intellectual powers weren't shaped only by coping with words on a page. Their parents may have enhanced their fluid intelligence by playing Tetris or learning the visual grammar of TV advertising. But that's child's play compared with Pokemon." Salute their metatrendy brains.

How Bad is Giving it Up For Good

Mukul Sharma

THE BURIAL SITES of early humans from the middle Palaeolithic period which starts as early as 300,000 years ago show not only that internment was often intentional but was also accompanied by ritual offerings at the gravesite, including flowers and other mortuary artefacts. This has been debated as demonstrating the origins of ritual practices and symbolic behaviour, but what is not controversial is that at some time very soon after this period religiosity became an integral part of the species. And that subsequently, though we may have evolved biologically, culturally and technologically, the belief in and reverence for a creator has remained with some 85 per cent of people right up to the present day.

Considering its duration and tenacity, some have suggested that such a belief structure must be an essential part of the human condition or psyche. Others have even suggested that perhaps there is some kind of 'god gene' operating or 'spiritual' aspect of DNA that makes us adhere to these convictions. Whatever the reason though, it's also generally supposed that the majority of human beings will continue to maintain their faith in a higher power either ruling over their lives or, at least, being responsible for original creation.

But the question is, how far into the future will they be able to sustain their belief, given the modern character of scientific progress and the exponential turn it's taken towards the computational sciences, artificial intelligence and robotics? In particular, how much of humanity can humans retain once they begin melding with machines? Or the other way around, when the very nature of prosthetics, synthetic organs and implants determine how much in us is actually organic and what parts non/natural? When the contents of consciousnesses can be downloaded to memory devices or uploaded from them into brains, it's going to be difficult to preserve the same self-image of our human wholeness.

Extreme technologies lie at the heart of this movement called transhumanism whose adherents view the human body as only work in progress and that the next dominant intelligence on Earth will be machines — which could, of course, be partly us. If that happens religiosity might be its first victim. By itself it isn't something calamitous or horrific but the real tragedy would be if it also means jettisoning our 300-millennia-old morality and concepts of good and evil along with it.

Timepass For the Watchmaker

Mukul Sharma

WILLIAM PALEY, THE 18th century Christian philosopher is famous for popularizing the Watchmaker Analogy or, as it's more commonly known now, the argument from design. Briefly, it goes thus: Human artefacts are products of intelligent design (or purpose) and the universe resembles such artefacts. Therefore the universe must be a product of intelligent design (or purpose) too. But since the universe is vastly more complex and gigantic than a human artefact, it must have been designed by a vastly more powerful and intelligent designer. In other words, just like the design of a watch implies a designer, so does the design of the universe.

The reasoning is so viscerally persuasive that despite advances made by science to explain complex phenomenon in terms of natural processes, its lure is still tempting. Thus if we say that the location of mountains can be described by plate tectonics or biological structures by natural selection and planetary systems by the nebular hypothesis, watchmaker proponents can always come back with: yes but these natural processes are the result of the creation of the universe. Which natural process created that?

Although the rebuttal may seem iron-clad, a fatal chink in its armour may now be developing through the field of cosmology which can strike it a death blow. Scientists are beginning to think that the Big Bang model of the creation of the universe may not be correct after all. According to some theories of quantum gravity everything in existence today could not have been packed into a singular point of infinite density, temperature and curvature. More importantly, they think that the current expansion of the universe was preceded by the collapsing phase of a previous universe which went through a Big Crunch and bounced out into this one.

Basically, this means everything was not created when scientists used to think it was but also existed before that. And perhaps before that too. This is where the design argument collapses completely because if a watch was never made but always existed, it obviously wouldn't require — or even imply — a watchmaker since only something that's been created needs a creator. So how do some faiths which also believe that the universe has always existed reconcile with their belief in a creator too? Simple: they say the creator has also always existed. In fact they rather imply that the two are inseparable aspects of each other.

Before the Twain Can Meet

Mukul Sharma

IS THE DIFFERENCE between faith and a conditional reliance on observation of the natural world so profound as to be completely unresolveable? It would seem so. As the statement of The Centre for the Study of Science and Religion puts it, sciences respond to a felt need to understand the world, and religions respond to a felt need for the world to have meaning. From these different starting points, one issue emerges at the junction of any science and any religion: are these felt needs commensurate? That is, is the universe a moral place and do things have a larger meaning than those we give to them? An approximate answer from any religion is in the affirmative and the answer from any science is negative.

Yet, a lot of people from both sides of the divide — including some perfectly well meaning individuals who may or may not be deluded — keep calling for a reconciliation of faith with empirical knowledge. If one looks into their agenda, however, one usually comes across a tacit resolve to ultimately subsume the other into its own perceived majesty. Scientists invariably mutter something along the lines of Einstein that true religion becomes ennobled and made more profound by scientific understanding, while believers quote only the first part of the same great physicist's statement that 'science without religion is lame' (the second part being, 'religion without science is blind').

The fact that this actually gets us nowhere can be seen by how both parties choose to employ the philosophical device called Ockham's razor. It's a principle attributed to the 14th-century English logician (and Franciscan friar!) William of Ockham which states that the explanation of any phenomenon should make as few assumptions as possible. In other words, go with the simpler explanation. But now watch the fun.

Which is simpler: an atheistic assertion that totally random occurrences led up to us, or a person of faith who believes it's all God's doing? If we go with the former then we have to accept that in order for the universe to exist there was this huge chain of unlikely events which created everything.

If we go with the latter then where's the extraordinary evidence that's always needed for an extraordinary claim? To arrive at any future reconciliation the first thing we have to understand is that these are not easy difficulties that can be papered over by liberal talk.

As Far Away From the Truth as Before

Mukul Sharma

WHEN DOES PERSONHOOD begin? There are problems on both sides of the divide. Pro-choicers — people who favour or support the right of women to choose whether or not to continue a pregnancy to term — believe that the transition from human life to human personhood is achieved part way through pregnancy, or perhaps at birth. But they do not believe that an egg that has been artificially fertilized in vitro by sperm and then allowed to grow for a few days till it consists of six to eight cells and subsequently frozen, are persons. They have no brain, nervous system, mouth, heart, lungs, or other internal organs; no organs to see, hear, touch, taste; they lack a body, head, arms, legs; they have no self awareness, memory, thought processes, or consciousness.

Such pre-embryos consist of a number of identical, undifferentiated cells which contain human DNA, much like a microscopic piece of adult skin from which, too, it's theoretically possible to clone a full-fledged human being. Thus, the value and status of a pre-embryo only lies in its ability for future development into a human person if it's afforded a proper process and environment.

Pro-lifers, on the other hand — those who advocate full legal protection of human embryos as persons — generally regard the start of human personhood as occurring at or immediately after conception. A strict pro-life position would, therefore, regard even the insertion of an intrauterine device that prevents fertilization of ova but can in some instances change the environment of the uterus to bar the implantation of a fertilized egg, as murder. Ditto emergency contraception like the 'morningafter' pill, medically induced abortions, harvesting stem cells from a pre-embryo which causes its death and discarding surplus pre-embryos in fertility clinics.

Interestingly, according to the *Bardo Thodol, The Tibetan Book of The Dead,* deceased souls who don't recognize the light of liberation in their post-mortem state, ultimately have karmically impelled dreamlike visions of copulating couples on Earth. At the instant an egg is fertilized they are supposed to have made their choice of parents and, thereafter, immediately enter and overtake the embryo for rebirth. Assuming this is indeed true, how would an incorporeal personal agency relate to cloning and in vitro fertilization? Would he or she have visions of the laboratory process instead?

Why it's Good to Be Alive?

Mukul Sharma

THE PROBLEM WITH trying to describe a universal morality is that differences in cultural traditions and customs filter down through social groups to ultimately operate in individuals. Thus, while in one part of the world honour killings may be sanctioned as morally advisable, in other places it's still murder. The same sort of questions even influence scientific research when the government of one country bans foetal stem cell research and another pushes for it. This notion of everyone having a different idea of good and bad, called Moral Relativism, is now being questioned by some scientists who feel they may be close to discovering a common basis for it.

Marc Hauser, author of *Moral Minds* and director of the Cognitive Evolution Laboratory at Harvard University, believes his research is adding credence to the idea of a 'universal goodness impulse' — just like there's also a universal language impulse. The impulse may generate different kinds of mutually incomprehensible speech patterns but the underlying stimulus remains the same. University of Maryland neuroscientist David Poeppel on the other hand feels that the moral rules we follow — such as when to do the right thing — is set in a sort of default position when we're born, like the factory settings on a PC, which form the basis of morality. Later the switches are set to particular values as a function of experience.

Like-minded researchers believe this so-called 'urge to good' must be universal because it's also seen in the altruistic behaviour exhibited in animals who often show an unselfish concern for the welfare of others. Most evolutionary scientists, however, refute the moral argument by saying that it's nothing but instinctive cooperative behaviour that may be detrimental to the individual but occurs nonetheless because it contributes to the overall survival of the species in the long run.

But this doesn't answer a far more fundamental question as to why survival itself should be deemed so important by all living things. What possible benefit could there be in making copies of our genes, ourselves or our groups? Saying 'survival benefit' is merely tautological. Obviously if it was bad to survive, nothing would have, even if it got infused with life somehow. Therefore, there's no getting away from the corollary that it must be good to survive. Why this is so is what science must now investigate.

The Science of Non-attachment

Mukul Sharma

THERE IS MUCH truth and even more to recommend what the expatriate Vietnamese Zen Buddhist monk, teacher, author, poet and peace activist, Nhat Hanh, has to say. During an interactive session in New Delhi he held, for instance, that the core of Buddhist teaching "is non-commitment to a view because by doing that you can become fanatical and create a lot of suffering."

Considering humankind's history of civilizational, social, domestic and interpersonal violence based on a variety of fanatically held beliefs, can anyone seriously doubt that statement? 'Views' in such contexts quickly degenerate into dogmas that have to be defended unto death by the faithful. The suffering is merely collateral damage thereafter.

Hanh, however, then goes on to say that one can come closer to the truth by looking at the nature of things. "To climb to the sixth step you have to abandon the fifth. And this can be done by non-attachment."

Now, while that may be true for most aspects of life, it could, at first, seem to have questionable value as far as scientific inquiry is concerned. One might think a scientist can hardly be expected to further the progress of knowledge if he or she abandons the previous step which is a necessary precursor to the next. But why bring science into all this? Because Hanh himself does. "A scientist needs to be non-attached as well," he says. "Because only if he's not attached to one truth, he can find another." We really know if Hanh had Einstein on his mind when he said that but if he did, he wouldn't be too wrong.

The great physicist got so fixated with some of the ramifications of his Theory of Relativity which gave one view of reality that he fought bitterly to the end of his life with the competing notions of nature thrown up by quantum mechanics. Today, we know that Quantum Theory is just as correct as Relativity is although it deals with a different aspect of reality — the microscopic, as opposed to the macroscopic.

Yet, for his time, Einstein too had to literally 'abandon' some of the earlier ideas of physics in order to come up with his revolutionary theories of matter, energy, space and time. The fact that some of these previous thoughts had been held sacrosanct for hundreds of years didn't mean he was not going to question their validity. When he did, they failed to hold fully and his jettisoning of some of them was justified by posterity.

The World Within Ourselves

Mukul Sharma

MOST OF US think of a hologram — the little thingies on credit cards, product packaging tags, etc — as just a high tech-three-dimensional image which is very difficult to tamper with. However, there's another extremely interesting property of holograms too: their entirety can be reconstructed from an arbitrarily small part. That is, if a hologram of a face is cut in half, each half contains all the information to make another — though smaller — image of the complete face. The same holds true even if the face is cut into a thousand pieces. In fact, a hologram is like a window with hundreds of panes; one can look at the same outside scene when it's fully open or through any one of its panes when it's closed. Every part of it contains all the information possessed by the whole.

Michael Talbot puts this in a different perspective in his book *The Holographic Universe*: The 'whole in every part' nature of a hologram, he says, provides us with an entirely new way of understanding organization and order. For most of its history, Western science has laboured under the bias that the best way to understand a physical phenomenon, whether a frog or an atom, is to dissect it and study its respective parts. A hologram teaches us that some things in the universe may not lend themselves to this approach. If we try to take apart something constructed holographically, we will not get the pieces of which it is made, we will only get smaller wholes.

Some people have used this argument to explain the curious quantum physics observation that under certain circumstances, so-called 'entangled' subatomic particles which were once together at some point of time, are able to remain in intimate and instant contact with each other even if they happen to be light years apart later. The reason is not that they're sending some sort of faster than light signals back and forth between them but because their separateness is in itself a false impression. At a fundamental level each is only an extension of everything it's embedded or immersed in — or vice versa.

This leads to a startling but staring-us-in-the-face conclusion that in reality there are no pieces that make up a whole because nothing exists which is not comprehensive by itself. Parts of things — like carburettors of cars or pancreas of people — are not unfinished business. Meaning, just like the universe harbours every one, each of us harbours a universe within ourselves too.

Are We Only on the Outside of Reality?

Mukul Sharma

IN 1982 THE French physicist Alain Aspect conducted an experiment that some people believe is one of the most important scientific events of the 20th century — one that has the potential to change our entire assessment of reality. Simply put, the experiment provided strong evidence that under certain circumstances subatomic particles such as electrons are able to instantly communicate with each other regardless of whether they were 10metres or 10billion kilometres apart. More importantly, it violated Einstein's edict that information can't travel faster than the speed of light; that there can be no 'spooky action at a distance' as he put it.

The late quantum physicist David Bohm, however, had a different take on it. He proposed that the observed electrons were not actually two separate entities but aspects of the same unity being manifest in altered viewing conditions. Think of an aquarium, he said, holding a single fish which we cannot see directly. Rather, we rely on images being recorded by two video cameras positioned in front and on one side of the aquarium. If one were to see the two video monitors one would get the initial impression that there were two fish inside the tank since the angle of videography would be different from two sides.

After a while, though, it might slowly start becoming apparent that there was some kind of relationship between the images. That, for instance, even while one fish appeared to face the front and the other was sideways, when the first made a movement or turn, the second always made a different but corresponding and simultaneous movement or turn too. Thus, if a person was unaware of the camera arrangement, he or she could easily come to the conclusion that the two fish were in some kind of direct and intimate communication with each other.

Therefore, according to Bohm then, the Alain Aspect experiment only reveals what is really going in the subatomic world of electrons and other such particles. The apparent faster than light communication between them is telling us there exists a deeper level of reality we are not privy to where such a 'pair' of electrons is only communicating with a part of itself. Or, to put it another way, the level of reality we are privy to is deceptive, misleading and, ultimately, illusory. And that all we ever know of the underlying reality are the ways in which it appears to manifest itself.

Evolution Can Coexist with God

Mukul Sharma

THE YEAR 2009 was the 200th anniversary of Charles Darwin's birth and the 150th anniversary of the publication of his *Origin of Species* which gave birth to the Theory of Evolution. Simply put, it states that change in the genetic composition of a population during successive generations as a result of natural selection acting on the variation among individuals results in the development of new species. In one brilliant flash of insight and sustained reasoning, Darwin demolished forever the idea that some divine creator made all the different species of animals and plants that have ever existed. A century and a half later, developments in the field of genetics and DNA have only confirmed the theory's basic tenets.

Of course, there's been resistance. In his own day Darwin was savagely attacked by people who felt threatened by what they perceived as not only a frontal attack on their fundamental religious beliefs but because evolution dethroned humans from their pedestal. No longer could man be considered the pinnacle of all creatures built for a godly purpose; he was just a blind by-product in the normal course of life's development. It was as shattering a blow as that delivered by Nicolaus Copernicus when his scientifically based heliocentric cosmology displaced the Earth from the centre of the universe to a bit player on the sidelines of one among billions of galaxies.

Even today, empirically illiterate creationists along with their so-called 'scientific' Intelligent Design contemporaries keep assailing evolution for being 'just a theory' which should be taught in schools along with all other theories of the creation of different species. In the process they conveniently forget that the Theory of Relativity and the Theory of Gravitation are also 'only theories'. They never attack those because who wants to jump off a building to prove one of them wrong.

So does this mean god cannot co-exist with evolution? Not at all. As far as believers are concerned they should understand that Darwin never attempted to explain how life itself first came to be nor how it originally arose from inanimate carbon compounds to become living matter. Darwin was also agnostic towards the existence of consciousness and mind. And till such time as science can explain such things they must remain the subject of philosophy and religion. Life can reach well beyond science, without coming into conflict with it.

Problems Within the Family Too

Mukul Sharma

SOMEONE WHO HAS not been your mother at one time in the past is not easy to find. Someone who has not been your father . . . your brother . . . your sister . . . your son . . . your daughter at one time in the past is not easy to find." It's a simple instruction for a happy life, a part of the Mata or Mother Sutra where the Buddha tried to show how the idea of rebirth can contribute to our compassion for others as well as give us a little comfort for ourselves. It's especially useful for those of us who can't inherently believe in an automatic extended human family without having actual ties of blood with them.

The world famous reincarnation researcher, Professor Ian Stevenson, who was also head of the department of psychiatry at the University of Virginia in the US and had conducted field work in Africa, Alaska, Canada, Burma, India, South America, Lebanon, Turkey, and many other places, found a curious connection here. Even though he personally believed there were scientific difficulties in accepting the hypothesis, he nevertheless found that people who claimed memories of another life were never geographically very removed during subsequent lives. That is, a person who currently lived in, say, Iran almost never claimed to have lived previously in some distant place like Iceland or Japan.

In fact, the one common thread running through all the anecdotal evidence was that rebirth took place within a radius of a few hundred kilometres at the most — either in another part of a large city or state or in another village down the road. Taken contiguously over a long enough period of time, this would obviously mean an increased likelihood of intermarriage and changing relationships amongst the particular population.

But forget rebirth; taken sufficiently back in time, this kind of interpersonal connectivity even begins to resemble a normal genetically linked biological model where, ultimately, everybody's related through a common ancestral link. It's something that was unthinkable before the 19th century prior to the advent of Darwin and Mendelian genetics. It's true, over millennia everyone's been mother, father, brother, sister, son or daughter to everyone else. Or will be in the future. That was a mark of the Buddha's prescience. Where he was off the mark was in assuming the existence of family ties could or would necessarily evoke compassionate behaviour in us.

Patterns of Sounds & Silence

Mukul Sharma

JOHN CAGE, A pioneer of chance and electronic music was, arguably, one of the most influential American composers of the 20th century. In 1952, he composed his quintessential piece, 4 Minutes and 33 Seconds which is totally silent with the score instructing the performers not to play their instruments during the entire duration. Cage's contention was that while no deliberate musical sound was produced, there would nonetheless be unpredictable and unintentional noises in the concert hall, home or head where it happened to be played. It is these sounds, he said, that are to be regarded as constituting the music in the piece.

But does complete silence really have any such significance on our hearing? Then how is it different from other silences? That depends. One story has it that a 7-inch vinyl version of 4'33" was at one time popular on the juke boxes of a number of bars as it gave customers a little relief from an otherwise relentless soundtrack of rock and roll. On an equally serious note, it's been used during funerals as a mark of respect to the gravity of the occasion without having interfering dirges being played in the background. It's also made extra money. A plagiarism suit against another performer who copied one minute of the original silence and then insisted it was not a quotation, was settled out of court for an undisclosed six figure sum in 2002.

Silence, of course, is not possible without sound but sound too — no matter how complex it might get in the course of either a sophisticated symphony or mobile phone conversation — is not possible without silences. The gaps in between invariably determine the fillings before and after and, indeed, often comprising them in ways which are not totally predictable. Of such stuff is also the *shunyata* or void of the universe composed. It is not an empty vacuum as traditional Western science once believed but gives rise, with fluctuations in that vacuum, to much matter and many worlds. A lot of scientists too are coming around to realize that the Big Bang of 13.7 billion years ago was not a one-off cosmic affair but part of something that's occurred several times in the future and will do so in the past again.

Right now, we and everything around us could well be one of those gaps. In which case, on either side of our 4 Minutes and 33 Seconds of silence lie sounds — fillings to fit in the fullness of the whole lattice.

Teaching the Other Side of Faith

Mukul Sharma

LEWIS THOMAS, SCIENTIST, poet, researcher and prizewinning author of *The Lives of a Cell,* once suggested in an essay, 'The Art of Teaching Science', that perhaps the best way to interest young people in science would be to teach them not only what was known but also what remained unknown. There should be, he said, courses dealing systematically with ignorance and informed bewilderment. Young minds should be told that every important scientific advance that has come in looking like an answer has turned sooner or later — usually sooner — into a question, and the game is just beginning. That, compared to the pond of knowledge, our ignorance remains oceanic and the horizon of the unknown keeps receding as we approach it.

"The conclusions reached in science," he wrote, "are always, when looked at closely, far more provisional and tentative than are most of the assumptions arrived at by our colleagues in the humanities. But we do not talk much in public about this, nor do we teach this side of science. We tend to say instead: These are the facts of the matter, and this is what the facts signify. Go and learn them, for they will be the same forever."

But let's see now; why do those lines — the last three in particular — sound so familiar? Yes, of course, it's because they're almost exactly what's said when religion is being imparted to young minds. That, this is what it is, this is what it means, this is what happens and this is indisputable. You have to interiorize such things as immutable facts that will bear no further uncertainty, indecision or question. They are eternal truths. Also, doubt is outside the pale of divinity and to question its beliefs is heresy. Yet, at the same time, intense faith is a deeply troubling issue as witness what was learnt about Mother Teresa, for instance, from her letter to a spiritual confidant: "...for me, the silence and the emptiness is so great that I look and do not see — listen and do not hear — the tongue moves in prayer but does not speak."

At a time when faith is being eroded — especially among the younger lot — perhaps the time has come to project the idea of religion more as Thomas suggested it be done for science: not as a grand anthology of unshakeable truths but more like a very rich but vastly unknown potential in our lives. Something that can be explored for discovery if one wishes to, instead of having the whole of it rammed down one's throat.

Just a Thinking Person's Reality

Mukul Sharma

THE FACT THAT most times we only perceive what we can conceive is dramatically borne out by what happened to Captain Cook when his ship reached the island of Tahiti in 1769. The Tahitians couldn't see the vessel even though it was moored directly in front of them. The reason a big sea-going craft like that was invisible to them was because they couldn't visualise such a structure, having had no previous exposure to something like it in all their experience, history, myths or imagination. As a result there was no modelling system available which could reconstruct its image with any meaningful correspondence to reality.

Even up to 70 years later, by which time a lot of missionary and other European ships had come into contact with the islanders, they still could only manage to describe ships as floating islands inhabited by beings of a superior nature, upon whose orders lightning flashed and thunder rumbled (the muskets and cannons on board). Today, a local Tahitian tourist guide can tell the engine difference between two brands of water scooters.

The philosopher Alfred North Whitehead also drew attention to this by saying that our conditioned mode of thinking and use of language affects our view of reality to such a great extent that it becomes virtually impossible for us to fully appreciate its magnitude. There are some fundamental assumptions, he said, which we unconsciously presuppose and these appear so obvious that people don't know what they are assuming because no other way of putting things has ever occurred to them. In other words, we can't really contemplate what we have no comprehension of, even if it is right in front of us. Therefore, the range of our knowledge of reality is limited by our preexisting beliefs and expectations.

Of course, having a consensus world view is a convenience since it's practical and has survival value. Nevertheless, it can be dangerous to forget that it's also a convenient fiction because when there's no new expectation, nothing new gets to happen and the 'out there' becomes falsely fixed. At the same time, the world that a bat or a shark sees is not the same as what we do and we blithely regard their interpretation of it as seriously flawed even though they survive by means of it just like we do with ours. Who's correct? As the physicist James Jeans put it: "The universe begins to look more like a great thought than a great machine."

The Age of Scientific Miracles

Mukul Sharma

A LOT IS being made of the survey conducted by the Institute for the Study of Secularism in Society and Culture of Trinity College in the US and Hyderabad-based Centre for Inquiry about the 'non-scientific' beliefs of Indian scientists. After assessing 1,100 scientists holding doctorate degrees from 130 universities and research centres across the country, the team found that almost half of them believe prayer is effective, 38 per cent believe God can perform miracles and 30 per cent believe in sins and deeds of past lives. Commenting on the findings, the chairman of the Centre for Inquiry, Narisetti Innaiah said: "Our scientists aren't applying the scientific temper in all fields of life to provide an ethical alternative to religious and paranormal worldviews."

But, really, what kind of ethical alternatives are we talking about here, when an amazing 64 per cent of scientists also said they would refuse to design biological weapons because of their beliefs, while 54 per cent said they will not work on nuclear weapons for the same reasons? Compare that with atheists and agnostics like J Robert Oppenheimer and Edward Teller who built the atom and hydrogen bombs which have in the past ended entire cities and in the future have the potential to end the whole world. If sensible people had a choice between them, religious extremists making mass destruction devices and the majority of Indian scientists surveyed, who should they choose?

That's not all. As many as 93 per cent scientists defined secularism as tolerance for other religions and beliefs, while only a minority said it meant atheism. A majority of scientists thought of themselves as being spiritual, which according to twothirds of them was either 'commitment to higher human ideals, such as peace, harmony or well-being' (34 per cent), or 'a higher level of human consciousness or awareness' (31 per cent). Are these convictions less important than merely possessing a scientific temper? What if one had such a temper and wasn't committed to the discovery of a higher ideal? Which would be preferable in interpersonal relationships or to society?

As for the 7 per cent of scientists who believed in ghosts, a Harris poll in 2003 found 51 per cent of lay Americans believed in them too. And that's an advanced country. In India the figure would be much higher. Obviously, the scientific temper must have worked miracles to lower the average so dramatically.

An Ontological Sense of Comfort

Mukul Sharma

IT'S FUNNY HOW the reactive human thought process generally works. You have a person who, say, spends his whole life debunking paranormal occurrences, exposing miracle working charlatans, poohpoohing UFOs, demystifying scientific mysteries and generally rubbishing everything from faith healing to flower therapy and almost everybody automatically assumes that he's got to be an atheist. As if every deeply religious person, on the other hand, is a complete idiot who has nothing better to do than to believe in alien abduction, astral projection and ectoplasm or that Uri Geller can bend a tablespoon by just thinking about it.

Martin Gardner, popular American mathematics and science writer specializing in recreational mathematics, but with interests encompassing stage magic, literature and religion and who was an outspoken critic of pseudoscience, ran across this same problem. He writes that when he disclosed in his *Whys of a Philosophical Scrivener* that he was, in fact, a philosophical theist — one who believes in God but is outside any traditional religion — it profoundly shocked readers who knew him only as a hard-nosed sceptic of psychic phenomenon and flying saucers.

Here's how this simplistic reasoning works in some of our minds: we equate a supreme being with everything that goes bump in the night and all that we believe is unexplained. And that since science cannot —and indeed doesn't even try to — prove the existence of

God and that, since science cannot — and, again, doesn't even try to — prove the existence of fairies at the bottom of the garden, they must both have the same basis for existing. We don't consider that some people may believe in God simply because of the sense of ontological wonder they get at finding themselves alive and don't question further.

Or as Gardner puts it: "I am not in the least annoyed because I do not understand time and space, or consciousness, or free will, or evil, or why the universe is made the way it is. I am relieved beyond measure that I do not need to comprehend more than dimly the nature of God or an afterlife. I do not want to be blinded by truths beyond the capacity of my eyes and brain and heart. I am content with the absence of rational methods for penetrating ultimate mysteries."

Now there's a comfort level most atheists and agnostics can't live with. Unfortunately, nor can the majority of believers.

Blind Faith Versus Scientific Path

Vithal C Nadkarni

DAMN ALL GENES to hell!" is her message on Face-Book. She is currently mugging almost round the clock for her biochem master's exam, so her ire is understandable. Her father, a scribe, shoots back immediately 'Please save some (genes) for the heart' on the social networking site. Why does this seem equally reasonable? While she's been slogging through her texts, he too has been up through the night filing a story on genes that regenerate hearts.

Of course, it's going to take years of painstaking work before that initial flash of discovery pans out, if at all, into a therapeutic gold strike! Ironically, it's the very sort of time-consuming work that the kid is going to train for her Ph D abroad. So she's earned the right to let off a bit of steam just as he has, to exult about an exciting discovery.

Beyond their harmless banter lie more contentious territories: here those who advise retreat into 'blind faith' clash with the plodders on the 'scientific path'. Emmanuel Kant was one celebrity who threw in the towel early on: In his second part of *The Critique of Judgement*, the transcendental idealist philosopher from Prussia declared quite boldly that it was quite absurd for man to make any attempts at taking on, let alone explain, 'the mechanics of life'. For it would be quite futile 'o hope that another Newton will arise in the future, who shall make comprehensible by us the production of a blade of grass according to natural laws which no design has ordered'.

If that wasn't enough, Kant rounds off the para with an even more definitive pronouncement: "We must absolutely deny this insight to men." In hindsight, the two brash youngsters who gate-crashed into the Nobel Prize party with their discovery (documented in their bestseller *Double Helix*) would beg to differ with our modest philosopher, as would the legions of scientists who went on to decode the entire human genome, the very alphabet of life, opening possibilities unimagined by our ancestors.

Needless to add, the jury is still out on whether Kant or his critics are right. Meanwhile, we mustn't ignore an explanation that harmonizes both points of view. This was developed centuries ago in the idyllic land of Kashmir by philosophers who taught that both enlightenment and enslavement of reason flow from one single universal reality. The trick lies in recognizing (*pratyabhijna*) it and to live in its light ever after.

What if There's Nothing in Between?

Mukul Sharma

QUANTUM INTERCONNECTEDNESS, THAT under certain circumstances subatomic particles are in some form of intimate connection with one another no matter how far apart they may be, is a fact of physics which few — if any — physicists can deny any longer. However, the implication of such an actuality renders the whole idea of space an illusion. If two things that were together once continue to behave as if they were still not separated by something we call distance then either 'oneness' doesn't exist or the gaps in between two 'ones' don't. In any case, it means the same thing — namely, the perception of an 'other' is also an illusion.

Scientists have discovered the existence of this phenomenon of entanglement as they call it by conducting actual experiments which have been accepted by their community. Interestingly, they can continue to conduct the same experiment on any one such pair of entangled entities today or one hundred years from now and still come up with the same result for that particular pair. This would mean that separation in time is also not for real and that time, too, must therefore be an illusion. Actually, this should come as no surprise since space and time are inextricably linked as Einstein said when he proposed space-time to be part of the same continuum.

Now, it's true that we're only talking about very small bits of matter that behave in such a bizarre counterintuitive way but then what are things like planets and people for instance made of if not these same infinitesimals? Can we really say that the nature of reality is completely different for the subatomic particles constituting our bodies than it is for the rest of our largeness? In which case where does the transition from to the other take place?

At the same time all around us we continue to see things separated by space and time: New York from New Delhi; Plato from Picasso. Could it be that we're living in a reality that's deliberately conducted differently from what it actually is and that we're only privy to the real thing by glimpses of it given to us by, say, mystics?

Well-known physicist Nick Herbert, author of *Quantum Reality* has this to say: "When we don't look at it the world exists in some strange state that is indescribable. Then when we look at it, it becomes absolutely ordinary, as though someone were trying to pull something over our eyes — the world is an illusion."

A Technological Leap of Faith

Mukul Sharma

THE SCIENTIFIC SEARCH for extraterrestrial (ET) intelligence has all the makings of a new religion. Believers argue that while it's true our Earth is the only planet in this solar system that harbours such life, astronomers in the last 15 years have already discovered some 400 other extra solar planets orbiting relatively nearby stars. What's more, they say, we haven't even scratched the surface. Considering our Milky Way galaxy alone has about 100 billion stars with potential intelligence-bearing life around them, and there are about 100 billion galaxies around, what are the chances — if not astronomical —that the universe is teeming with sentience?

Unbelievers are not convinced by such blind faith. They like to paraphrase physicist Enrico Fermi's paradox which states that although the size and age of the universe suggests many technologically-advanced civilizations ought to exist, the hypothesis seems inconsistent with the lack of evidence to support it. In other words, if ETs exist, then where the heck are they? Why have we not heard from them? Not a single alien space probe has ever been seen or contacted and, in any case, if travel is difficult for them, why have we not been able to detect any of their radio transmissions at least? Why the great silence? Unless there's nothing to hear and no one out there.

Agnostics point out that the search for alien intelligence has been in progress for at least 50 years with increasing powerful instruments being pressed into service searching for electromagnetic signals but, to date, nothing definitive has emerged. However, they also point out that seeking something in our image is being rather human-centric; other intelligences don't necessarily have to be housed in humanoid forms, using bodily processes or homo sapient technology. Therefore, without ever-knowing what ET could be like, we can never take it for granted that we will find it or it even exists.

Faith, as usual, plays a big part in this belief or unbelief system. The US government at one time funded the search for ET through a Nasa programme with federal grants, just like it once funded research into faith healing too. Human beings like to believe in belief, and often it works for those who believe the hardest while the faithless take faith in only themselves. Yet, does anyone really like to think we've been cast adrift alone into the unknown?

On What's Sacred & What's Not

Mukul Sharma

PLAYING GOD IS something science has to deal with all the time. So how should we, the people supposedly out of its ambit yet enjoying the benefits of technology, deal with it? Was food meant to be eaten uncooked by flames? Are we only supposed to use our legs for locomotion? Is the written word an unnatural form of communication? In other words, what is natural? Can we seriously say the 19th century British philosopher John Stuart Mill was wrong when he wrote in an essay called 'On Nature' that the term 'natural' was one of the most copious sources of false taste, false philosophy, false morality and even bad law?

In more recent times, in vitro fertilization, or the creation of test tube babies using a process by which egg cells are fertilized by sperm outside of the womb and then re-implanted into the mother, caused a worldwide furore when it was first introduced in the late 1970s. Today fertility labs offering such facilities operate literally out of corner clinics which commuters — some of them the kin of people who immolated themselves protesting such monstrously unnatural horrors — routinely pass on their way to work. In another instance, the world seemed to wake into a unanimous nightmare of disgust when Dolly the Sheep was initially cloned. Most of us were fast asleep to the same concern when she died seven years later in 2003.

And so we'll sporadically continue saying 'some things are sacred' for a long time (till they magically stop being so) and give the yuk response against genetically modified foods, designer babies and euthanasia without realizing that all around us in increasing walks of life we've finally begun to play God in the exact way He is supposed to have done when playing us.

That's because computers have become far too ubiquitous and inevitable to be considered morally unacceptable any longer. At the same time the fact that it's only a matter of decades now before artificial intelligence begins matching ours and surpasses it, is easily overlooked. If it wasn't, we'd appreciate that, for better or for worse, science may have played God for the last time and handed over the baton to new forms of intelligence to develop their own playing fields of the future. That's when we'd probably also have to ask ourselves the question: Were our sciences actually meant to play God in order for us to become gods ourselves? Meaning, is nothing sacred? Including us?

Another Story, Another Moral

Mukul Sharma

A HARE ONE day ridiculed the slow pace of the tortoise, who replied, "Though you be swift as the wind, I can beat you in a 100metre race if I be given a 10metre headstart." The hare, believing this assertion to be a complete no-brainer, agreed. During the race the tortoise never for a moment stopped, but went plodding on with nary a halt in his stride straight towards the finish line. The arrogant hare, confident he would win in any case, decided to catch a little shut-eye in between. At last waking up, he saw his opponent had almost reached the goal and, run as fast as he might after that, he was never able to overtake him.

Now, only an idiot tortoise would challenge a hare to a race in the first place, right? So what was this famously slow moving reptile thinking when he decided to take on such a fleet-footed mammal? New studies have shown that there was no way the tortoise could have known the overconfident hare would take a short nap that would spell doom for him. Besides, when the historic event took place the proverb 'slow and steady wins the race' hadn't even been invented.

Today scientists realize that actually the tortoise was exceedingly well-read in the ancient Greeks and was relying on something called Zeno's paradox in order to outfox his opponent. He figured that if he had a 10metre headstart then in order to overtake him the hare would first have to cover the 10metre distance. But by that time he himself would have moved, say, a metre ahead. So the hare would have to then first cover that one metre. But by that time he would again be ahead by, say, a tenth of a metre which the hare would have to cover next and by which time he would be ahead by a hundredth of metre and so on. Forget overtaking the tortoise, the hare wouldn't even be able to ever catch up with him.

For hundreds of years thereafter people thought the quickest runner can never overtake the slowest, since the pursuer must first reach the point whence the pursued started, so that the slower must always hold a lead. In a recently held 'rematch of the millennium' a much more modern hare who was well-versed in calculus which has shown the paradox to be wrong, easily outran a deeply disappointed descendent of the original tortoise. In an interview later he mourned, "Mathematics just ain't what it used to be." Moral: All scientific progress comes at a price.

'Wild Saints' Worthy of Worship

Vithal C Nadkarni

IN THE 1960s, the veteran grizzly expert and wilderness enthusiast Doug Peacock went to Vietnam as a young army medic. The searing experience changed his sensibilities forever. After his return, the war veteran, otherwise known as 'cranky buzzard', found himself utterly out of sync with urban America. So he exiled himself to the wilderness which he found to be 'less wild than I remembered'. He set out to save it with the help of the eco-enthusiast Edward Abbey: the duo happily 'monkey-wrenched' wilderness-gobbling schemes such as logging and land development.

Their adventures inspired Abbey's cult classic novel *The Monkey-Wrench Gang*, which immortalized the peacock-turned-buzzard as a character called George Hayduke that was 'a night-time trouble-maker, bar-room brawler, free-time lover'. Shrugging off that image as 'literary licence', Peacock today prefers to focus instead on his life's mission, namely, making the world safe for grizzly bears.

The bears turned out to be his healing wild shamans. The towering creatures could have easily killed and eaten him up; yet they had the grace to let him out of situations where they would have been within rights to swat the blundering veteran's head off.

Peacock is convinced that human intelligence itself evolved in response to being a relatively puny animal hunted by what American nature writer William Quammen once described to your correspondent in an interview as 'God's Monster' — massive alpha predators such as the tiger, the lion, the Klondike Bear and the Great White Shark. Our collective survival still depends on the world's wild places in a real way, he says. For without these animals there would be no context for fear, he adds.

The hardcore wilderness groupie is obviously too disdainful to include smooth-faced suicide bombers and their dead-eyed handlers in his list of hunters that strike terror in the hearts of the hunted. In any case, their breeding grounds are in conurbations. What makes them deadlier, however, is the sheer banality of their evil. This stems not from any instinct for food or survival but from a twisted ideology that dehumanises their anonymous victims and denies the very rights and freedoms that the terrorists allegedly espouse, and which they arrogate to themselves as 'God's chosen people'. In comparison, the carnivore stands out as a wild saint worthy of worship.